WRITING AND SELLING SCIENCE FICTION

WRITING & SELLING

SCIENCE FICTION

BY THE SCIENCE FICTION WRITERS OF AMERICA

Writer's Digest

9933 Alliance Road · Cincinnati, Ohio 45242

94168

Library of Congress Cataloging in Publication Data

Grant, C. L.
Writing and selling science fiction
1. Science fiction — Authorship
I. Grant, C. L.
PN3377.5.S3W7   809.3'876   76-25893
ISBN 0-911654-35-6

Writer's Digest
Div., F&W Publishing Corporation
9933 Alliance Road
Cincinnati, Ohio 45242

Contents

words, back up. Study drama. Listen to strangers. And take a long look at your characters — maybe your dialogue sounds tinnish because your characterization is thinnish.

INTRODUCTION:

Getting Your Feet Wet

This volume is a tool. But, like those tools in the workshops of other types of craftsmen, it is not intended to be an end in itself, but only a means through which you, as a new writer, can create a final artistic product — specifically, a self-contained, polished, hopefully marketable piece of fiction. This tool (or volume, if you prefer) does not carry with it a lifetime, money-back guarantee that you will become an instant success after reading it, nor does it hold out the ethereal promise that you will grind out salable material each and every time you sit down at your typewriter. But it does combine the considerable talents of some of the foremost authors in science fiction and fantasy to guide you into the creation of SF, and to show you where they, like the rest of us newcomers, made their mistakes — so that you will be all the wiser for knowing them, and all the more clever for avoiding them.

Theodore Sturgeon, in what has come to be known as Sturgeon's Law, has stated that ninety percent of all science fiction is pure drek. The same, of course, could be said for any other genre in fiction ... but it doesn't necessarily have to be that way. A little care, a lot of caring, a lot of study will enable you to avoid most of the pitfalls and many of the annoyances that give editors headaches, and you rejection slips.

You will be reading articles whose primary function is not to *tell* you what and how to write, but to *assist* you through the sometimes frustrating maze that is artistic creation. From James Gunn's analysis of plot and plot ideas to Kate Wilhelm's incisive exploration of character development; from Jerry Pournelle's examination of logical future societies to Gardner Dozois's focus on their inhabitants. Further, there are essays on the noncreative side of fiction writing, on the hardware a writer must be aware of before he can successfully see his story into print — e.g., Thomas Monteleone's guidelines for submissions, markets and agents, and andrew j offutt's extremely practical hints for savings in paper and ribbons, and for what to do when the taxman wants to know where you're getting all that extra money.

The consummate genius, of course, needs little instruction beyond the mere mechanics; but that same consummate genius is just as rare in science fiction as in the outside world. For the rest of the fraternity of authors, writing is hard work. Hard work, long hours, fits and starts of depression, disappointments large and small, loneliness ... these are unwelcome companions indeed, but they are an integral part of this mysterious process of artistic creation, and they have been and will continue to be discouraging, defeating, and unpleasantly constant sources of nightmares and self-deprecation.

And yet, paradoxically, they also make up part of the magnificent challenge that is creating good fiction.

Believe it or not, it's true.

And just to prove that not all new writers eventually wind up with filing cabinets and closets stuffed with the debris of Sturgeon's Law; with typewriters whimpering forlornly under a mantle of dust in the corner; with reams of unused paper wrinkling under the bed — I'm going to give voice here to my ego and show you me: the best example I know of someone who did in fact get his feet wet and did not drown.

I would like to share with you a few rules that I learned the hard way; rules that are almost always obvious when they're pointed out to you, and hideously hidden when they're not.

Rule #1: READ. READ. And when you're tired of READING, READ AGAIN.

I know exactly when I began to write seriously (which is to say, for publication, glory, and millions of dollars). It was in 1966, and the goading came — as it has to countless others — when I read a story in a so-called teenage magazine, and declared rather pompously to myself that I could easily do much better than that, if only I wanted to, would bother to, and had the time to. The attitude here is, I'm sure, instantly recognizable: it lends a falsified air of self-importance to one's untried and untested talents, and it can and does develop into an insidious, reverse snobbery that prevents thousands of would-be authors from daring to take that chance to see if indeed "I could do better."

Unlike the would-bes, however, I did eventually allow that story to goad me into trying. If, I thought, that particular editor could let something like *that* story cross his desk, then I would give him something that would knock the publishing world on its collective pins and make the critics stand up and cheer.

And whatever you think was the result of this effort — you are absolutely right.

My initial foray was a short-short entitled "Jenny, Jennifer," a naive attempt at explaining how young people learn their prejudices. It was, to be charitable, an absolute failure on all counts, and yet it remains to this day my favorite story — not because of its tremendous characterization, or incisive probes into Man's psyche, or its elegant poetry; it remains my favorite because, after I had received the fifteenth rejection slip from magazines ranging from *Playboy* to *Guideposts,* I finally forced myself to sit down, grit my ego's teeth, and tear the stupid thing apart. And in doing so, I discovered quite painfully that I hadn't the vaguest notion as to what went into the actual creation of a short story.

That's when I began to read.

I snapped up magazines like *Writer's Digest* and read all I could on the mechanics of creative writing, the formats for submissions, and so forth. I rifled the library for books on the same subjects, and more. I read, studied, hit myself over the head for my stupidity, and when I thought I finally had the hang of it, I next had to decide what *kind* of story I was going to (try to) write.

There really was not much choice in the matter. Today, as in 1966, the prime market for short fiction is the SF/fantasy field. The old testing grounds for new writers — *Collier's, The Saturday Evening Post, Story Magazine* — have either faded into nostalgia or are mere shadows of their former selves; nonfiction has taken over, even in the book industry, and fiction is being driven out. SF: where else are there so many regular magazines and original story anthologies competing for an author's wares?

So. Seeing this as my big chance, I wrote four stories in rapid succession, uncovered editorial addresses, and sat back to await the checks and the plaudits.

Again, you're ahead of me and you're right. Nothing. Not one blessed thing. More stories, more nothings. And all I received for my creative pains were those blasted little printed letters which thanked me kindly for my submission but noted that it did not meet the current needs of the magazine. I learned to hate those words. Intensely.

Thank heavens, then, for Frederik Pohl.

I had sent him something called "Strawberry Flare," and when he returned it, there was a short, handwritten note at the bottom of the rejection slip. When I finally deciphered his scrawl, Fred was telling me in no uncertain terms that perhaps I should read his magazine — *Galaxy* — before I tried to sell to him again.

A simple suggestion — so simple that I, like many others, had overlooked it until nearly too late. It goes without saying (he said) that if a new writer doesn't know the field he's trying to conquer, there's no way he's even going to find the battlefield. If I didn't know anything about engineering, who would hire me to build a bridge? Similarly, if you do not know what SF writers are doing today, you're certainly not going to convince an editor to part with his company's money for something he hasn't purchased in 20 years.

So back I went to the newsstands and the libraries, and I picked up all of the SF magazines I could find, and I read them. More. I studied them. And I discovered several important things that have not since changed: that the movies I was seeing in my local theatres bore little or no relation to the contemporary printed SF — from *Attack of the Crab Monsters* to *The Beginning of the End,* they were all shams and I had fallen for their fakery. That the same was and is true of television SF — studying *Lost in Space, The Six Million Dollar Man,* or even the majority of shows in the *Star Trek* series won't give you, the writer, anything but eyestrain.

Back to the bookstore and the newsstands, then.

I read current science fiction and science fact, and renewed my acquaintances with Shakespeare, Dickens, Hardy, and all the other masters of human observation and characterization. And listen: when your eyes are opened, you're staggered by the wealth and education in what you used to think was boring simply because it was labeled "classic."

Armed, then, with this fantastic array of new knowledge, and with that which I had picked up in the very act of writing, I returned confidently to my typewriter and promptly fell over. . .

Rule # 2: *DISCIPLINE THYSELF.*

A telephone call interrupts my work, not once but several times, and I spend an hour or more talking with a friend (lady or otherwise) while a story dies slowly on the platen vine;

I get stuck with a hitch in a plot and instead of thrashing it out or moving to another piece to clear my mind, I wander off to watch some television, wash the dishes or take a long walk — all of which effectively destroys that particular work period;

I begin working at six on Monday, 8:30 on Tuesday, nothing at all Wednesday through Friday, maybe a couple of hours here and there on Saturday and Sunday.

As I look back, trembling, on this rather haphazard thing I would hesitate to call a schedule, I am amazed that I was ever able to complete a coherent sentence, much less finish a story from beginning to end. But somehow I did. There were the usual false starts and bogged-down middles, but there were also several that blundered into final drafts, vanished from my mailbox and returned just as rapidly as those I had written before discovering Rule # 1. My ego (and more about that little creep later) took a fearful pummeling, and I began nursing a suspicion that perhaps my bravado was covering the fact that I lacked sufficient talent; maybe, I thought, I should stick to declaring that I could do better, and let it go at that.

I distinctly remember an autumn Saturday when I was struggling to remember part of a paragraph I had begun sometime earlier in the day. There was a phrase I was searching for, and I knew I had had it once; and then I knew what was wrong. Again, a simple solution not always obvious when you're sitting on it, blindfolded. If I had stayed with my typewriter while the words were coming, if I hadn't answered the telephone or whatever it was, I would have been able to complete the paragraph, and the story.

Dumb was the mildest thing I called myself that day.

A schedule, then, with a definite set of parameters, and an admonition to stick to it no matter how painful it became. The same hours every night, every day, all and every week. The phone calls, the walks, the trips to the kitchen and to the corner store were unmasked as excuses for not working.

That the schedule was effective, exceedingly so, was brought home to me later when I discovered that when I was not at home during the appointed writing times, I actually felt *guilty!* I think I even apologized to the typewriter when I did get home, promising to make up the lost time. The funny thing is ... I made it up.

And that guilt contributed toward my improvement as a writer because it eventually kept me at my infernal writing machine long enough to learn

Rule #3: WRITE, EVEN WHEN YOU HAVE NOTH-ING TO SAY.

Ray Bradbury has said that although he has had published around 300 short stories, there are easily ten times that many mouldering somewhere in his study. He is not alone. I can assure you that there are in my files more stories that never saw the end of the first draft — or even of the second paragraph — than I have ever dreamed of publishing in my lifetime. On my shelf are pitiful attempts at novels that I wouldn't dare show to my best friend, novelets that make me cry whenever ill fortune makes me stumble inadvertently over them.

A bitter pill to swallow: not everything you are going to write will be a ray of the purest gem serene. Even Shakespeare had his moments of hackwork and trivia.

But neither are these failures complete in the absolute sense; if you are indeed serious about writing (and if you're not, what are you doing here?), you can learn from those unoriginal ideas, the poor and shoddy construction, the absolutely grotesque novella you ground out the day before yesterday. You have to hold back the tears, sometimes, but you can learn if you want to.

For one thing, those monstrous mistakes can keep your ego in its proper place. When you begin to believe that there's nothing you can't do with ribbon and key, check out a few of your earlier attempts to rock the world. Lesson: Shakespeare wasn't perfect, and neither are you.

Your early stories can also serve as a fair measure of your professional growth, and act as a spotlight for your weaknesses. Why were they either rejected continuously or never sent out? Unrealistic and stilted dialogue? Plots with holes big enough to snuggle around Uranus? Cardboard characters who shred as soon as you poke them, searching for a little spark of humanity? An unbelievable planetary atmosphere that wouldn't sustain a rock, much less your aliens? Save what you write, and study it.

If you only set down 100 words during those lonely (and they are that, you know) writing hours, those 100 words could mean the difference between a sale and another lousy rejection slip.

I have several notebooks filled with papers — and some papers have only a single line on them, with more notes in the margins than words in story sequence, with lists of phrases that might make good titles (if only I could hang a story on them), with sentences that sound like fantastic endings of stories I've never written because I couldn't figure out how to get there.

None of this is wasted time, however.

If you do not have an instant story idea floating around in those pages, *practice a little, practice a lot!* Write some dialogue, and don't worry about where it's going — just sharpen your ear so that what's put down on paper is what you want the reader to "hear"; rough out a paragraph or two of description, even if it's only of that kitchen sink with two weeks' worth of dirty dishes spilling over onto the floor. Focus your writing eye so the reader will be able to "see" what you are talking about (and this is particularly true of character description: Gorn's mighty chest "heaved" with anger — "heaved"? To heave means to throw, folks. Watch your vocabulary). Do all this and you'll not only sharpen your writing senses (to the eternal benefit of your fans) and get practice in just plain typing, but you also might discover yourself falling into a story you didn't even know you were going to write. In addition, I have found that working this way (when ideas are hard to come by, that is) has helped me to exorcise clichés from my writing vocabulary and has given me much needed practice in developing the skills necessary to write one story in first person, another in third.

The gimmick, of course, is to train yourself, to make your fingers automatically curl into position whenever you sit down in front of your magic machine. And it's definitely a most rewarding way to give yourself a little writing education.

Which brings us to

**Rule #4: OBSERVE, EAVESDROP, AND OTHER-
WISE TUNE YOURSELF IN TO WHAT'S
GOING ON AROUND YOU.**

While there is always room for argument (*discussion,* if you prefer) about which tricks work for one writer and which work for another, I have never in the short time I have been in the field met an author yet who does not practice his profession 24 hours a day (and twice on Sundays).

It may come as a surprise to some of the newer folk out there (as it did to me) that the typewriter makes up only a small portion of what we so blithely call the creative process. Sure, you can round up a bunch of chimps willing to work for practically nothing, and stick them in a room with a clatter of typewriters; and sure, they will eventually pound out between banana peels the complete works of Charles Dickens with all the grammar and ghosts intact. But they are performing a purely mechanical act that has no bearing at all on the world outside.

You want to create things (stories, novels, plays) that *live!* To make your people real, then, to make your readers believe and care for the characters in your world (villains or heroes, it makes no difference), you have to learn about and understand the flesh-and-blood folks who trundle by your house every day, every week, all year. You don't have to hand out detailed questionnaires to them, but it certainly wouldn't hurt to plop yourself down on the stoop and watch them. How do they walk? How do they hold their hands when they talk? How do they hold their heads when they are angry, happy, melancholy, joyous? Do they talk to themselves? Whistle? Grunt? Forge dead ahead with their eyes on the sidewalk, sky, traffic? Clothing, mannerisms, degrees of involvement with their surroundings, physical and mental attitudes can all be observed and transferred to the printed page, if you will become a constant people-watcher. If not always a conscious one.

You do not have to say to yourself, for instance, that the guy in the mauve caftan waiting for the bus is going to be in your next story (though that has been the case in at least one of my own), but the impressions your mind receives from his very existence will be filed away and can be brought back later when you need them, even if you don't remember where you got them in the first place. Characters do not spring full-blown like Minerva; they are the direct result of synthesis, and the more you observe, the more fragments you can choose from in order to make a more realistic whole.

There are tricks, too.

Give yourself a fifth limb, an extension of your mental awareness: an ever-present notepad. When and if something strikes you, and you want to insure that you will not forget it, write it down. Now. Don't delay. And if people stare at you — and they will, believe me — smile and keep writing. Remember — you know something they don't.

Sit in a restaurant, diner, movie theatre, whatever — listen without shame (if you won't tell, I won't) to the conversations around you. When I was a teacher, I made the mistake of telling one of my creative writing classes that I stood outside the classroom door before and after each class to eavesdrop. Somehow the word spread. Traffic diminished greatly for the next few days, and everybody spoke in whispers. But despite such obstacles, and assuming you don't make your eavesdropping obvious, you'll be able to store away patterns of speech, accents, dialects, mannerisms of voice, intonations of emotion and a dozen other dimensions that will add to your characters' credibility. It's common knowledge, in fact, that more than one story has resulted from a snatch of dialogue overheard at an airport, train station, or bus depot.

And at the risk of repeating myself for the umpteenth time: When something strikes you, write it down. No matter how clever and eidetic you may think yourself, *please do not rely on your infallible memory! It is NOT INFALLIBLE.* As sure as the sun is going to come poking up through that smog every day, you are going to forget it. Do not trust yourself. Ever. *Write it down!*

And speaking of that notepad, I owe a great deal to Jerry Pournelle who kept insisting (and keeps insisting — I don't believe that he believes that I've taken his advice) that I keep a sheet of paper and a pencil next to my bed for those midnight inspirations. I could probably retire right now if I had a dollar for every idea that came to me while I was drifting off to sleep, and faded into remorse the following morning — all because I thought that it was such an absolutely magnificent idea, such a sure-fire seller and award winner, that I fell asleep grinning and counting the royalties and the cars and houses I would buy with it.

And forgot it.

It all comes down to this: you are a creator — and that's what you are, friend, so don't let anyone tell you differently — and as such, you just cannot afford to pass up anything that will possibly enhance your abilities. If it seems like too much trouble, then you are in the wrong business.

People-watching and eavesdropping are only two ways, however, that you can educate yourself in a way that no book, this one included, can ever top. After all, there are just so many hints I and the other writers can give you before you have to strike out on your lonely own and DO. Therefore, be aware, too, of your environment. Do not take what you think you know about your neighborhood for granted — you know less than you think. Observe and study the trees and their seasonal changes, the buildings, the avenues, the traffic, the countryside — once you begin observing shape, you'll notice immediately that no two scenes are ever exactly alike at any given time of any given day in any kind of weather. What will eventually distinguish you, the writer, from the rest of humanity, will be your heightened ability to mark these subtle changes and set them into print.

Finally, there is a single, underlying factor to all that has gone before in this Introduction, and it is

Rule #5: If you don't want it badly enough, don't waste your time.

Several times throughout this piece, I've mentioned a thing called ego. For our purposes — and most especially, yours — ego here has little to do with conceit, either for one's talents or one's stature. Ego is the image you have of yourself as a writer. It is a necessary adjunct to your creativity, and unfortunately, it is wide open and vulnerable to infliction of all manner of pain. When someone — an editor, friend or critic — tells you that a particular story you have spent hours and days and weeks struggling over is not the best fiction ever to come barreling down the pike, it is going to hurt. When an editor says he would like the first five pages rewritten to take the space of only one and a half, it is going to hurt.

Stories, you see, are going to be your children, whether they are 5,000 or 50,000 words long. And anyone who is going to put down your children is asking for a fight.

Many authors will say repeatedly and loudly that critics do not bother them. I cannot believe that this is entirely the case. Sticking my neck out, I think that what they are actually saying is: I have constructed a protective pod around my ego which, while it doesn't prevent me from learning through constructive criticism, it does keep me from leaping out of the nearest window every time a harsh word hurtles in my baby's direction.

But that same ego will also tell you, through an indefinably instinctive process, that what they, and I, and you are doing is *good*. Sometimes, the story is merely competent (though competency takes a long time to achieve regularly, if it is achieved at all); on the other hand, that ego will whisper that this story here, right here, is really, fantastically, out-of-this-world *GOOD!* You *know* it. You can *feel* it, *sense* it when the final word is typed and that *—30—* is tagged onto the bottom of the last page. You are totally convinced of it when you send the story prayerfully off in the next day's mail. And, if your self-critical abilities have been properly, realistically developed, that story will in fact be good, and salable, and eventually sold.

But to keep this ego in perspective, and to keep it alive, you must want to write. And not the same kind of "want" that has you sighing over that six-month trip through Europe, panting every time you pass the Mercedes showroom. It's the kind of "want" that will literally force you to stay awake at night thinking of plots; taking out that pad in the middle of a restaurant without self-consciousness; snarling every time you get a rejection slip and sending the story out again, and again, and again.

There isn't anybody writing science fiction today who doesn't want to.

Harlan Ellison has said any number of times in any number of places that writing isn't solely, or even primarily, a matter of having to meet your car payments with a new novelet or the mortgage with a new novel — one writes because one can't *not* write; and that, I am convinced, is the difference between the man who sells only one story every five years, and the man who is a true author.

Take it from me — and I am still a new writer — that once you have experienced that indescribable sweetness that comes with seeing a story of yours in print for the first or the dozenth time, you will know that there is no other sensation quite like it in the world; and if you are bound to be a writer, you will also know that you cannot do anything else and still be as happy.

It can't be done.

Way back at the beginning of this Introduction, I mentioned dear old "Jenny, Jennifer," my first and most lovable failure. I also mentioned some of the rules I follow; some I found out the hard way (on my own), and others were given to me by fellow writers who know what it is like to start out with nothing but a typewriter and a blank piece of paper. Well, those rules brought me much pain and much euphoria. In 1968, I wrote a pastiche of horror stories solidified by the Gothic mold. It's called (for those of you with poor memories for trivia) "The House of Evil." I sent it to Ed Ferman, editor of *The Magazine of Fantasy and Science Fiction.* He sent it back with a note, asking me to cut down the first two pages. *Pain,* my friends, but by that time — even though I hadn't yet made a sale — I needed to write. I took a day off from work, rewrote the beginning and sent the story back. A week later I received a check for $100. Two years later I made my second sale. A year after that, my third. Now it's up to 28, two Nebula nominations, two novels, panels at SF conventions, and once in a while, a fan letter.

But I am still a new writer. I am still learning. And I still suffer through all those miserable rejection slip syndromes of depression, disappointment, disgust and deprecation.

The trouble is, you see, I am addicted to the stuff.

The delight is, I got my feet wet and I didn't drown.

The Kick of It

Postscript: the rules I have set down rather imperiously are, of course, tailored to suit my peculiar circumstances and my very peculiar temperament. They are, of necessity, generalized and overlapping. Some of them may work for you, and the rest definitely will not. Which rules will assist you, as a new writer, will depend on the kind of person you are and the talents you have waiting to be exploited.

Similarly, the articles that follow this rambling frequently overlap in their suggestions, and in some cases, might even contradict each other. This does not imply invalidity. Again, remember that we are dealing with a combination of your personality and of the personalities of 11 authors.

Unlike any other professionals I have seen in the world, writers want to help writers. Believe me, there's room for everyone in the pool.

So, by the time you have finished this book, you will have discovered that writing is not a disconnected series of isolated contrivances pieced together in the form of connecting paragraphs ostensibly called a story. Everything in fiction is umbilical to everything else; idea, dialogue, character and plot do not exist independently of each other. A short story or a novel is a mosaic in which all parts fit perfectly, or not at all. Your job as a beginning writer is to learn how to make them fit, and fit well; to bolster your admitted (and don't forget to admit them!) weaknesses with your strengths until you strengthen that which is weak.

Read.

Write.

Discipline.

Observe.

WANT!

It's not as simple as all that. You know it already (or will learn to recognize it). I know it, having been thumped on the head with it for the past decade.

But believe it or not, it is fun. And rewarding in more than monetary terms. And if you want to get the kick out of it that I do, then

Why are you reading this? Get back to your typewriter and WRITE!

— C. L. Grant

Thomas F. Monteleone *is one of the newest and best science fiction writers working today. He has sold over two dozen short stories and novelets, two novels (Seeds of Change — Laser Books; The Time Connection — Popular Library), and numerous articles and book reviews in professional and amateur science fiction magazines. He is currently working on a novelization of his popular Chicago stories and a scholarly book on the life and work of Roger Zelazny.*

The following article is based in part on his work as reader and assistant editor for Amazing Science Fiction *and* Fantastic Stories. *He is splendidly qualified to pick up on the most common mistakes new writers make in submitting their first works, and in answering some of the more common questions concerning markets, agents and other nuts-and-bolts problems which a new writer must surmount before he can break into the science fiction field.*

CHAPTER 1:

Science Fiction Markets: Where and to Whom?

by
Thomas F. Monteleone

To write good science fiction and sell it, the writer should familiarize himself as thoroughly as possible with the genre. Many beginning writers (*and* some professional "mainstream" authors) who are not familiar with science fiction think that the genre is a source of easy money and that one can sell a science fiction editor virtually anything that is semiliterate.

Nothing could be further from the truth.

Sadly, people who are not familiar with modern science fiction still harbor images that ceased to be valid almost 40 years ago: lurid cover art featuring half-nude women and bug-eyed monsters, fleets of ornate spaceships, and hosts of mad scientists. The motion picture industry (excluding such notable exceptions as *2001: A Space Odyssey* and *Forbidden Planet*) has perpetuated this false impression of SF with an unending number of poor films. But these clichés have been absent from modern science fiction for several decades.

How, then, does one become familiar with contemporary SF? The answer is obvious: read it. Most libraries have extensive science fiction collections, and an interested reader can find enough books to provide a sufficient overview of what is being done in the genre today. Some recommended titles include: *The Science Fiction Hall of Fame, vol. I,* edited by Robert Silverberg; the *Nebula Award Stories, vols. 1-9,* by various editors; *The Hugo Winners, vols. I & II,* edited by Isaac Asimov; *Modern Science Fiction,* edited by Norman Spinrad; and the annual *World's Best SF* anthologies that were edited by Terry Carr and Donald A. Wollheim. The majority of the collections concentrate on the short story and novelet lengths of fiction; but they are extremely useful, since most writers break into the field by selling short fiction first. The novels usually come later.

Another source of good current science fiction is the SF magazines that may be found on the larger newsstands throughout the country. As I write this, there are five monthly and bimonthly magazines: *Amazing Stories, Analog, Fantastic Stories, Galaxy,* and *The Magazine of Fantasy and Science Fiction.* These publications are digest-sized and contain short stories, novelets, serialized novels, articles, book reviews, and spirited letter columns.

As the writer reads these magazines and becomes familiar with them, he will discover that each has its own distinct personality which reflects the tastes and preferences of its editor. For example, several of these magazines (like *Analog*) specialize in stories that are highly extrapolative, emphasizing the "hard-science" aspects of SF; a few of the others (like *Galaxy)* concentrate on stories that are more speculative; while still others (like *Fantastic*) publish fantasy material that places little emphasis on scientific principles or ideas. Probing the personalities of these magazines becomes immensely important to the beginning SF writer; he can thereby avoid sending a story about a nuts-and-bolts technician to an editor who prefers protagonists that are Emersonian romantics, or vice-versa.

The science fiction magazines, then, are a reliable and steady market for stories of all lengths, although most editors prefer shorter stories from newer writers. The magazines appear regularly and thus require a constant influx of new material, but this does not mean that it is easy to sell to them. Actually, the reverse is more true.

For the past four years, I have been a contributing editor for *Amazing Stories,* writing book reviews and reading unsolicited manuscripts. During that time, I have become thoroughly familiar with the way unsolicited material is winnowed out or bought. *Amazing* receives around 450 manuscripts per month (mostly from unpublished writers); and that figure is fairly close to what the other four science fiction magazines receive each month. Of the initial 450 stories, between 60 and 70 percent are immediately rejectable for various reasons: poor writing ability, lack of plot, clichéd plot, stereotyped characterizations, unresolved conflict, etc. Another 30 to 35 percent are also rejected, but perhaps because they lack only one important aspect of narrative that makes a good story. These manuscripts *do* show promise. Their authors are encouraged for exhibiting some degree of talent. The remaining five to ten percent of the unsolicited material is not returned immediately to its authors. These stories — perhaps ten to 15 manuscripts in all — are passed on from the first reader to the editor; and from this batch, the editor may select one or two that will eventually see print. In other words, most of the science fiction magazines buy less than one half of one percent of all the unsolicited manuscripts they receive.

At first glance, such odds may seem impossible to overcome; on second consideration, perhaps things are a bit brighter than they seem. Short fiction in most non-SF markets is scarce indeed. Consider the words of Damon Knight, discussing the fate of the short story in his delightful book of criticism, *In Search of Wonder;*

Cramped and constricted as it is, the science fiction field is one of the best of the very few paying markets for a

*serious short-story writer. The quality magazines publish
a negligible quantity of fiction; slick short stories are as
polished and interchangeable as lukewarm-water faucets;
the pulps are gone; the little magazines pay only in prestige.*

In addition, the few magazines that do publish contemporary
(or mainstream) fiction are swamped with *thousands* of submissions each month; there are many more writers attempting
to sell current fiction than science fiction. In short, then, the
odds are better trying to sell science fiction than any other
type of fiction.

Let us now assume that one succeeds in selling a story
to an SF magazine. What kind of payment can one expect
to receive? The rates vary from one magazine to another,
with factors such as the quality and length of the story helping
to determine the final rate of payment. The average science
fiction magazine pays around three cents per word, although
beginning writers may expect one or two cents per word, and
an established professional may command as much as four
or five cents per word. The first story I ever sold was about
3,000 words in length; I received $30 for it. A beginning writer
selling a 5,000-word story to one of the magazines may expect
to receive a check for $50, or at most, $100. The payment
schedules also vary among the different magazines. Some of
them pay upon acceptance, while others do not send out their
checks until a story has been scheduled for a particular issue.
Still, this is better than the situation at some of the pulp
magazines in the thirties, when payment, as one wily old SF
writer is fond of saying, was upon lawsuit.

What rights are purchased when a magazine editor buys
a science fiction story? The policy is fairly standard. In most
cases, the magazines buy the right to print a story one time
(presumably the first time) in North America; and this is
commonly called "first North American serial rights." There
are variations on this standard agreement, however. Some
publications may ask for "first world rights," which gives them

the right to publish a story for the first time abroad. If a magazine buys "all rights," that means that the writer relinquishes all subsidiary use and sales of that story: reprints, anthologies, radio & TV, motion picture. It is recommended that the writer attempt to retain as many subsidiary rights as possible.

The Anthology Market

In addition to the SF magazines, however, there is another large market for short stories — the original anthologies. Although these original short story collections (as opposed to reprint anthologies) have been extant within the field for decades, only within the last several years have they become a large market. Forty-two original anthologies were published in 1974 — in direct competition with the magazines.

Currently, two major types of original anthologies are being published. The first is the *series anthology*, which is a continuing collection of books under the same general title, such as *Orbit, Universe* or *New Dimensions*. This type of anthology is very similar to the magazine concept, although it appears only once or twice a year, usually in a hardcover edition. The stories, like those of a typical magazine issue, will be of various lengths and themes — and each story is a totally individual effort. The only bond that these stories share is that their editor feels that they are well-written and consistent with his personal definition of good science fiction. Currently, there are a number of series anthologies that have survived for many years, and have gathered faithful readerships. Such anthologies are also a good steady market for short fiction. But remember, as one becomes familiar with them, he will realize that series anthology editors, like magazine editors, have their own likes and dislikes; each collection will have its own recognizable personality.

The second type of story collection currently popular among

publishers is the *theme anthology,* which is a single edition containing stories that explore a central idea. The possibilities for anthologies of this type are practically limitless. Some themes that have been recently investigated include the relationships between humans and aliens (*Fellowship of the Stars,* edited by Terry Carr); the fate of future urban environments (*Future City,* edited by Roger Elwood); and even speculations on the future of sex (*Strange Bedfellows,* edited by Thomas N. Scortia). Depending upon the quality of the material submitted, this type of anthology can be either a bright success or a dismal failure. There is the constant danger in a theme anthology that the stories will sound similar since they are all concerned with the same basic idea. A discerning editor, therefore, will buy only those stories that are highly inventive and original. The rate of payment for both series and theme anthologies is generally a bit higher than for the magazines: between three and five cents per word. And there is a chance for additional money if and when the anthology is sold for paperback publication — and it almost always is.

But how can you become aware of these potential markets? After all, the editors of such story collections do not advertise for material in the monthly writer's magazines such as *Writer's Digest,* or even in the annual listings such as *Writer's Market.* There are actually several places where the beginning science fiction writer can find such anthology markets listed. The first is the official publication of the Science Fiction Writers of America, *The SFWA Bulletin.* This bimonthly magazine contains an extensive "Market Report" which lists all current anthology and book projects in need of material. The Science Fiction Writers of America is a writer's guild for *professional, published* SF writers, and it issues *The Bulletin* to all members free of charge.

Peddling the Novel

Another science fiction market has traditionally been the novel. Although most science fiction novelists have broken into the field by first selling shorter fiction, some writers have preferred to engage their careers by concentrating on novels from the outset. There is a host of book publishers interested in good, salable science fiction, and most of them are listed in *Writer's Market*. However, some book publishers release more SF titles than others. In 1974, the largest hardcover publishers of science fiction, in descending order of books released, were: Doubleday, Putnam's, Harper and Row, Walker, Random House, Hawthorn, Seabury Press, Simon and Schuster, Macmillan, Dutton, Trident, Chilton, Scribner's, and Thomas Nelson. Perhaps 20 more publishers released one to three titles, but they were not among the leaders. Doubleday, for example, published 28 SF novels and collections in 1974; Putnam's published 18.

There is also a great number of paperback companies that publish science fiction novels. The largest of those include DAW Books, Ace Books, Ballantine, Dell, Berkley, Avon, Bantam, Signet, and Pocket Books. Another publisher, Harlequin, recently entered the science fiction field, and planned to issue 40 original titles in 1975 — making it one of the larger markets for science fiction.

The payment for SF novels varies among different publishers, although there are some average figures that can give the writer some idea of what to expect for a manuscript between 50,000 and 70,000 words. The average hardcover publisher offers an advance against royalties of $1,500 to $2,500, depending upon the length of the manuscript, the name of the author, and the size of the audience it expects to reach. The average contract will offer royalties of around ten percent of the book's purchase price for perhaps the first 5,000 copies sold, escalating to 12½ percent for all copies over the original 5,000 sold. Paperback publishers are now offering advances similar to the hardcovers, although the top figure may average out closer to $2,000 for newer writers.

The greatest difference with paperback novels is that the writer can usually expect to sell a greater number of copies. While the average hardcover science fiction novel may sell around 4,500 copies, a paperback SF novel may be expected to sell between 50,000 and 60,000 copies during its print run. This means that the contract from paperback publishers may have a smaller royalty percentage – perhaps six to eight percent. However, this is more than adequately compensated for by the larger volume of sales in the paperback edition.

There are several ways of marketing a science fiction novel. The first is simply to sit down and write a manuscript of approximately 60,000 words, look up the address of a possible publisher, put the novel in a sturdy carton, and mail it off to the editor. Be sure, as with the submission of shorter fiction, to include sufficient postage for the manuscript's return in case it is rejected. This whole process is known as writing novels "on spec," i.e., writing an entire novel before one has an editor either interested in it or already obliged to purchase it. I know several writers who work this way, and who claim that they have no regrets about writing in this manner. However, there are more desirable (and in the long run, more economical) ways of writing science fiction novels – especially for the newer writer.

If one has an idea that he feels would make a good novel, he should first send a *query* to several editors. A query is nothing more than a short note describing the intended novel, and asking whether the editor would be interested in seeing an outline and a few completed chapters. This technique saves the writer many months of work on a book-length manuscript that (1) is difficult and expensive to send through the mails and that (2) represents hours that could be spent on other material if the novel is unacceptable. If an editor responds favorably to his query, the writer needs only to compose an outline of perhaps eight to 15 pages which sufficiently details the major points of action and plot. Some writers prefer to write an outline called a "synopsis," which is a highly condensed version of the intended novel in narrative form; others prefer the more familiar chapter-by-chapter format that displays the story in the form of a book. Usually the writer uses the technique with which he is most comfortable. At any rate, the writer should then attach several sample chapters — usually the beginning few plus one from near the end of the book — so that the editor will have some idea of what the completed manuscript would be like.

If the editor likes the outline and chapters, he will usually offer the writer a standard publishing contract which offers the advance and royalty agreements discussed before. The contract will also have stipulations regarding subsidiary rights. The average book contract will have percentages for both the writer and the publisher regarding subsidiary rights; and although it is difficult for beginning writers to haggle over which rights are assigned to whom and in what percentages, it is always recommended that the writer try to retain as many rights and benefits as possible.

Once the writer has signed and returned the publisher's contract, he will usually receive half of the proposed advance on the novel. It is at this time that the writer can confidently finish his novel, knowing that when it is completed, he will have a publisher waiting to rush it into galleys. The remaining half of the advance is received when the author delivers the completed manuscript. I feel that this is by far the most preferred way to market and sell science fiction novels; the advantages are obvious to anyone who wants to save time and energy. In addition, queries, outlines and sample chapters are a good way of becoming personally acquainted with editors. For the editor, the beginning writer thus ceases to be just another name on the title page of a manuscript in the "slush pile." The editor remembers the writer's name and may be more inclined to consider his future queries or submissions.

To learn what kinds of novels are being purchased by today's science fiction editors, the beginning writer should sample some recent novels which can be found in the paperback racks of the local bookstore or in hardcover editions from the library. He may also study durable and excellent science fiction novels by reading the titles listed in the appendices of *The Hugo Winners,* edited by Isaac Asimov, and *Nebula Award Stories Nine,* edited by Kate Wilhelm.

He might also dip into the field of science fiction criticism. By understanding what some of the genre critics have to say about previously published SF works, the new writer will have a firmer grasp on what mistakes he should avoid. One of the earliest but finest critical works on science fiction is *In Search of Wonder* by Damon Knight, which explores the strengths and weaknesses of many of the better-known science fiction authors and their works. Two more recent works of criticism, *The Issue at Hand* and *More Issues at Hand,* by James Blish (writing as William Atheling), also deal with a variety of science fiction stories and novels; they are useful tools for new writers.

The Scoop On Agents

Aside from the magazines and the book publishers, there are also the related markets for science fiction, such as radio, TV, and of course, films. Within the last few years, there has been an upsurge of electronic-media interest in SF, and increasingly authors are seeking their stories and novels being optioned to television studios and motion picture companies. But the beginning writer will have much difficulty breaking into these lucrative markets. Unless the writer has already published a fairly large backlog of successful material, or lives in Hollywood where he can work directly with producers, or has an agent to do this work for him, it is unlikely that he will be successful in Hollywood markets.

This brings up another important aspect of marketing

science fiction to the magazine and book publishers: the literary agent. Who should use an agent — and how and when? There are no easy answers to these questions, but there are some guidelines that the beginning writer may wish to follow. In science fiction, there is only a handful of literary agents familiar enough with the genre to operate successfully. Most of the science fiction authors who employ agents are usually represented by these agents who are on speaking-and-lunch terms with most of the magazine and book editors who handle science fiction. There may be hundreds of literary agents who will handle SF, but I would recommend dealing only with those who have demonstrated the most competence and experience within the genre. Good science fiction agents can be instrumental in getting the writer new book contracts, foreign sales, translations and reprint sales. Agents are, of course, extremely helpful in selling a writer's material to the editors with whom they meet and speak frequently.

But the real issue is: *When* does a newer writer actually need an agent? And the truth of the matter is that most agents will not handle unpublished writers since, frankly, the amount of time invested in trying to sell their material does not net a profitable return for the agent. The standard commission for a literary agent is ten percent of whatever he sells for the writer/client. Therefore, the agent only wants authors who can consistently produce salable fiction. Most writers do not need the services of an agent until they are writing and selling so much, so often, that they simply do not have the time to bother with marketing. Most beginning writers do not have that particular "problem," and thus, do not really need the services of an agent.

In conclusion, allow me to include a few helpful tips which may mean the difference between an acceptance and a rejection slip. Always include a self-addressed stamped envelope (S.A.S.E.) for a manuscript's safe return. Editors receive a large volume of submissions, and they lack the time, postage and inclination to send back material that is not properly submitted. If a writer feels that a cover letter is necessary to introduce a story, he should make it brief and to the point. Rambling letters of explanation and (believe it or not, I've received them) self-praise only serve to turn off an editor. Ideally, of course, a cover letter should only be used to make note of previous publishing credits that an editor may be otherwise unaware of. Another important tip is always to be sure that the *science* in one's stories is valid, i.e., based on present theory or fact. Editors despise stories that rely on jargon and pseudoscientific explanations for story events. And finally, be sure that you know a market before submitting material to it. H.L. Gold, one-time editor of *Galaxy,* used to proclaim that no one had ever sold him a story who had not been familiar with his magazine. He was probably correct.

Selling science fiction is a stiff challenge for a new writer; it is hoped that a careful study of the various markets, and an intelligent application of what is learned from that study, will allow the good writer to be successful.

Recommended Reading

Asimov, Isaac. *The Hugo Winners, vol. I.* New York: Doubleday, 1962.

Asimov, Isaac. *The Hugo Winners. vol. II.* New York: Doubleday, 1971.

Blish, James. *The Issue at Hand.* Chicago: Advent Publishers, 1964.

Blish, James. *More Issues at Hand.* Chicago: Advent Publishers, 1970.

Carr, Terry, ed. *Fellowship of Stars.* New York: Simon and Schuster, 1974.

Carr, Terry, ed. *Universe 1.* New York: Ace Books, 1972.

Carr, Terry, ed. *Universe 2.* New York: Ace Books, 1973.

Elwood, Roger, ed. *Future City.* New York: Trident Press, 1973.

Knight, Damon. *In Search of Wonder.* Chicago: Advent Publishers, 1967.

Knight, Damon. *Orbit 14.* New York: Harper and Row, 1974.

Scortia, Thomas N., ed. *Strange Bedfellows.* New York: Random House, 1973.

Silverberg, Robert. *New Dimensions II.* New York: Doubleday, 1972.

Silverberg, Robert. *The Science Fiction Hall of Fame, vol. I.* New York: Doubleday, 1970.

Spinrad, Norman. *Modern Science Fiction.* New York: Anchor Books, 1974.

Willhelm, Kate, ed. *Nebula Award Stories Nine.* New York: Harper and Row, 1974.

A major and continuing complaint from the SF magazine editors runs like this: "This would be a fine story if only the characters had more dimension than the rocket ships."

Science fiction has changed. Today, an editor/publisher demands that manuscripts contain people rather than cardboard constructs; and there are few working in the field today who are the equal of **Kate Wilhelm** *in creating living characters.*

Kate Wilhelm is the wife of SFWA founder, Damon Knight, has written dozens of stories and novels, and has won many top honors and accolades in and out of science fiction. Her story, "The Planners," won the Nebula Award for short fiction in 1968.

CHAPTER 2:

On Characters
by
Kate Wilhelm

Two of the many ways to approach stories are: work out the story and then people it with appropriate characters; have the people first, and discover their story. These are totally different approaches, but in either one the characters must come alive and be unique, or the story will fail.

Let's take the first method. Suppose the story being developed is about a plague that threatens a major city. New York has been overused; let's say the city is Atlanta. The writer has researched the details of the plague; he has the city map and has visited the city and knows something of its atmosphere. The story is ready to write, except for the characters. Obviously there will be doctors, nurses, public health officials, police, politicians and some victims. The easiest way to proceed now is to reach out and pull in a Doctor; anyone in a white coat with a stethoscope will do. A Nurse to stand at his elbow and hold a tray; a woman in white. And so on. Now the writer has his characters: a Doctor, a Nurse, a Politician. . . . It might make a television series, or a movie, but it won't make memorable fiction.

In order to get beyond the stereotypes, the writer must think about the characters as if they were alive, complete with past histories. Let the Doctor be a person who has worked nights and weekends from the time she was 14. She was educated on full scholastic scholarships, has two older brothers who bullied her as a child, lost an early love, and has a friendly if not passionate marriage. Now she is a person, not just a Doctor. She will react as a human being first, a doctor second. She will get headaches, have her teeth filled when necessary, perhaps bite her fingernails and collect maps of exotic places. A *person* has something at stake in the story now, and is far removed from the institutional Doctor. Most of this background won't be used directly in the story, but it will be a powerful influence on the writer dealing with this character, and this will show.

A person who grew up an only child, indulged by parents, sickly, brilliant, is not going to react to situations and other people in the same way as one who was robust, outgoing, one among six children. Someone who was slapped around as a child will have a different world view than someone who never was touched in anger. How can anyone know what the characters are likely to do or say without knowing something of their background?

Giving characters real backgrounds will also provide them with a consistency of behavior. Our woman doctor is not going to wait for others to smooth the way for her — no one ever did so in the past; she wouldn't expect it now. There will be certain, almost reflexive responses to situations in which she feels she is being bullied — she had to learn to cope with her two brothers quite early. She knows how to get along with males without having to think about it — she has succeeded in a field that is 90 percent male. There will be a consistency in her actions that arises from her childhood. Even more important: if the writer has this kind of information about his characters, he knows when their tolerance level is approached, when they will erupt into atypical behavior. If this woman, at 13, became so angry at one of the brothers that she pushed him out of a window, she is likely to resort to some kind of direct physical action later in life when she feels threatened. If she pouted and wept and became ill, her anger is now likely to become inner-directed.

Someone whose ancestors were from the deep south is going to show influences that are different from New York's, or the northwest's, or California's. There are subtle influences working on all of us all the time, and the longer one has lived in any area where regional views are strong, the more one is going to reflect them. One obvious difference is in the speech patterns, inflections, syntax — down to the choice of words.

There are restrictions inherent in this plot-first method because the story will determine the characters possible for it, and often they are defined by their occupations. It is perhaps logical to use this method when the characters are secondary to the plot, or the ideas. The puzzle is worked out: a locked room, or space problem, or whatever. Now someone has to find the solution — a detective, or an astronaut. Since it is much easier to find a model for an astronaut or detective in fiction than in real life, most of the characters we see in these roles are interchangeable. Chances are we'll remember the particular puzzle long after we have forgotten the characters, but chances are even better that we'll simply forget the whole thing.

The trick is to look behind the uniform or occupation to the person. The hero must spend 23 hours each day not doing something heroic, after all. When he is not being a hero, what is he doing? Why is he a hero? For money? To prove he is not a coward? Family pressures? If the writer knows the answers, the hero is not just another cardboard doll being manipulated through the actions, but a person with a past and a future, one hopes. If the hero dies, some people will weep for him and suffer loss. Others will chortle with glee. He cannot be independent of the world he lives in and be human.

Often these stories will not be very complex, or have much richness or depth, because the actions possible for the characters have been predetermined by the plot necessities. If the writer recognizes the limitations and works to overcome them by giving the characters as much attention as the plot twists, the fiction can be good, and it is practically guaranteed to be well received. Good strong adventure with real people is a rarity.

Quizzing a Stranger

The other method of writing fiction is to start with the characters and go through them to the story. A number of years ago a question and my answer to it made me realize that this is how I work. The question was about a character of mine, and my answer involved her parents, her brothers, where they went to church, how they entertained themselves — in fact, nearly everything about them that could be stated in a few minutes. It was more than the question demanded. I realized I had created not only a young woman, but her entire family, although they played no part in her story that I was telling. I had sketchy information about her parents' backgrounds, and, more firmly, an idea of what her brothers would be likely to do with their lives. I took it for granted that this was the proper way to handle fictitious characters because it was the only way I could do it; and I was shocked to learn that not all writers work like this.

I think it is generally conceded that much of any creative process is unconscious and unknown; whenever we say "This is how I do it," we are actually saying, "This is what I understand about my own processes." What I am aware of in my own process of writing is that first there is a person, or more than one person, presented to me visually in my mind. I am fully aware of the emotional state of the person — anguish, elation, fear, whatever —— and I could describe her or him physically. There is little else. Sometimes there is a detailed background; often there is not. I have a person who is in emotional turmoil and who is more likely than not to be on a bare stage. But it is at that point that I know a story is going to be written, and I know it because the person I have seen has touched me very deeply. It is this quality of emotion that I strive to recreate in whatever story I then discover and eventually write.

There is no story for a long time while I'm investigating the character I have glimpsed. There are questions to be answered before I can know what story this character has. Most important: do I like him or her? What do I feel toward the character? How did he or she get here? From where? And so on. I find new scenes appearing that present the same character interacting with other people and again the scenes will be brief, but if they are right, they will fit the emotional set that has been established by now. Meanwhile I am unraveling the original character as much as possible. Is he a lawyer? No. A doctor? No. Salesman? Maybe. Married? Yes, but not happily; a happily married person has that to fall back on, and doesn't suffer anguish to this extent. It is like picking pieces of a tangled line, now and then getting one that will draw out, hitting knots with others that refuse to come undone, finding loose ends with yet others and discarding them. And all the while, I'm learning this character, singly or in combination with others.

At this stage it is like meeting a stranger and being entirely free to quiz him or her fully. As a writer I am free to inquire into the most intimate details of this new life, and gradually I find I am involved in a new process of elimination. This is not going to be a story about robbery, not about marital troubles, not about many things. The circle is closing on the possibilities open to this character. This is where the past reading, the storing of bits and pieces of oddities, comes into the picture.

In the case of my story "Somerset Dreams," I had been

reading a lot about dream research, and it seemed natural to work it into the story; but until there was a character who came to life, there was no story line, not even a suggestion as to how I could use the knowledge I had been acquiring. The story grew out of the character, her past and her future.

This story began for me when I visualized a young woman walking down the center of a ruined street. She obviously didn't live in that small, almost deserted town; her clothes were wrong, her attitude was wrong, everything about her was wrong. Working through her I discovered she is a professional woman living in New York, home for a short time only. Why? This led me to her childhood, her parents. Her mother is dead, her father a cripple. She is trying to decide if she should move back home and care for him here among familiar surroundings.

Again and again I have found that this method works for me. In "The Funeral" the story started for me when I saw a young girl walking along a spotless hall. She is dressed in a grey uniform, her hands clasped before her, her eyes downcast. Her hair is drawn tightly off her face. Why? Who would do this to a lovely young girl? Who is she? Why is she afraid?

A Human Repertoire

So we have these two methods of starting a story, and in each there are the same difficult questions to be answered dealing with the characters of the story. No doubt there are many other ways, but whatever the approach, the character has to be learned, cross-examined, dissected and understood — or the story is not going to work on any level except the most superficial.

As long as the character is the writer, there is no problem of knowing how to treat him or her in various situations. The character simply reacts exactly like the author. But if the character is someone else — and the most difficult other is the opposite sex — problems do arise. We have to distinguish here between the basic emotional states of human beings and their overt actions. The differences lie not in their psyches but in their behavior, and if this is really understood and accepted, careful observation will give the writer what he needs to write any character.

Someone asked me a long time ago what I knew about murder, passion and hatred. A character of mine did in fact commit murder and my reader correctly guessed I had had the same thoughts myself. Of course I had, and so has everyone else. Fictitious characters in all their glory and their ignominy have to come out of the writer, disguised in various ways; but they are bits of the writer or they don't breathe, don't live.

The writer who is afraid of revealing himself is missing the whole point. Our own experiences seldom are pure, uncluttered by mundane events that have nothing to do with them; they usually exist simultaneously and tend to rub the edges off. Time dilutes our experiences; we repress parts of them. And most important, we don't know along the way how much each one will influence the rest of our lives; we can't know until we lie on our deathbeds. Fiction permits us to follow cause and effect in a purer form and allows us some understanding of the human condition — but only if the author has been honest and has used his own emotional states or instinctual drives to motivate his characters. These, if true to the author, will be true to the character and to the reader. The range of behavior will be very wide, but the motivating forces are our own.

Suppose you are in charge of five preschool age children, all from the same family situations, with the same number of siblings, etc. At the last minute you tell them you have changed your mind and will not take them to the circus. They all feel the same anger and disappointment, even betrayal, but one throws a tantrum; one has an instant stomach ache and vomits; one pouts and weeps; one draws on the walls, spills milk, steps on the cat; and one shows little of anything, but wets the bed that night. Here are demonstrated five different ways of reacting to anger and frustration. The same people 20 years later will continue to cover a wide spread of reactions to identical situations.

That example does not even mention the sex of the children, because at that early age it plays little part in their displays of emotions. Heredity and the home are the shaping factors, but cultural influences make up the third force eventually. Cultural mores determine what responses are permissible for males and females, and they are different.

There is a traffic jam. All traffic is stalled for miles. Some men get out and walk to the source of the tie-up; women remain with their cars. Some men become angry and possibly start a fight with the inept driver at blame; women smoke more cigarettes. Some of the men leave the scene, drive down a steep bank, lurch over rough ground to get around the accident; women wait for the road to be cleared. These are all responses to the same situation, the same feelings about it: anger, impatience, curiosity and so on.

The difference is determined by what society says is acceptable. In order to develop awareness of these differences in overt behavior, the writer has to observe all the time, under all kinds of conditions, always noting how he or she would have acted and how the people involved are actually acting. Gradually a repertoire of human behavior becomes available that can be drawn upon at will. The combination of the writer's own feelings — drives, fears, needs — and the observed behavior of himself or herself and of others make up the two halves of good characterization.

Also one should remember that even though half a dozen people are doing the same thing — say, climbing a mountain — they are doing it for different reasons. Knowing the why behind the character's actions determines how the character is treated. Someone who would rather die than be thought a coward is going to behave differently on the snowy slopes from someone who is along to collect ecological data. There is tension between them even before the first word of the story is on paper.

Getting Physical

Nowhere have I mentioned physical descriptions, mannerisms, ages of the characters; there is a reason. If the writer knows the characters thoroughly, all this will come through without effort. It is when no more than the physical description is available that the writer tends to go in for heavy detailed descriptions of the way one character parts his hair, or another does her fingernails. Besides, unless the character has a gross abnormality, the description that fits him or her will fit millions of other people as well.

What we remember about people is how they behave: a violent temper, or loving personality; funny storyteller; good mimic; reserved or warm; arrogant or humble . . . . We don't remember people because they are or are not tall brunettes.

Another reason for not going into this part of characterization, except as a cautionary warning, is that there is a tendency in bad writing to use the spit-and-clap-your-hands methods of characterization. In this the character always spits before he speaks, or claps his hands with each speech for emphasis, or picks lint, or does something else equally meaningless just to establish in the reader's mind that this is indeed the same character who spoke three lines before. If the writer needs to ladle out this kind of reminder, he is in the wrong business.

What I want from fictitious characters is a consistent psychology, and real emotions; and from these I can construct my own images. It has been a disappointment many times to see a movie made from a novel I liked, and find all the characters are just wrong. I have shaped them in my mind where they exist as real people and the Hollywood versions are almost always imposters.

Some people write brief biographical notes about their characters, i.e., born, Chicago, 1957, brown hair, blue eyes, Northwestern U., etc. It can't hurt anything. Any device that forces the attention onto the character is worthwhile. I sometimes write down a series of dates, especially with characters who are older than I am, just so I can remember if they could have seen the Chicago Exposition of 1903, for example. Usually I live with my characters for a long time that varies, depending on whether it is a novel or short story I am working on: during this period of getting acquainted, I learn about the character's home, the clothes he or she likes, the favorite foods, music, amusements — everything I can find out. By the time I'm ready to write, I know the person as well as I know any good friend, and I don't need notes any more than I would need notes to write a short biography of my husband or one of my children.

No doubt there are many other ways to approach the problems of bringing to life an entirely fictitious being, but this is the way I work, and the only way I can begin to understand. In summary it is this: know your characters as if they were living people — and then *write* them as if they were living people.

Too often in SF stories and novels, the characters speak as if through a glass, darkly, woodenly, with little emotion or realtion to the real world. **Gene Snyder,** *whose career includes advanced degrees and college professorships in drama, offers for the new writer a brief history of dialogue, and how to use it most effectively in a story so that it not only brings the characters to life, but also aids in developing plot, establishing setting, and underlining effective scene description.*

CHAPTER 3:

"Dialogue?" "Of course!" "But how?" "You'll see."
by
Gene Snyder

"Dialogue helps, by God! In fact, it does more than help. Dialogue carries action, lubricates the mechanism of the plot, develops and enriches characters and provides exposition. Without the chisel of dialogue, you'd have to sculpt that short story or novel with your narrative mallet alone."

I've given this speech to writing students many times. A disturbingly large number of them come to me and say they feel "funny" about writing dialogue. Many of them can't think what their characters should say to one another. Still others find that they can't get in and out of a scene.

Because there's a strong strain of Dramatic Literature in my background, I tend to point them in the direction of drama for some degree of solace. I tell them that dialogue is the *only* tool the dramatist has to create action. Drama has employed dialogue almost exclusively for nearly 2,500 years, while the novel has used it for nearly 500 and the short story has chimed in only since the early nineteenth century.

The Dramatists invented dialogue and took thousands of years to perfect it. They honed, polished and shaped the interchange of conversation until they could move an audience to pity, terror, tears and laughter simply by having a few characters speak to one another on a stage. I tell students to read a play or two, or ten. Then, there's a good chance that they'll find the "why" of dialogue. And, in that "why," they'll find the roots of the "how."

The Proper Blend

It's clear that having the characters on a stage is substantially different from having them on the printed page; and in that respect, the playwright has more to work with than the novelist or the short story writer. However, there is little question that the latter has clear advantages that the former does not. The writer of nondramatic fiction has the capability of creating exciting dialogue and mixing it with narrative.

In the mixture of the two, the modern fiction writer creates a stew of various ingredients. It helps to see the narrative as the stock, and the dialogue as the meat and vegetables. Alone, either of them is bland. Together, they can be a tasty dish.

When the proper blend of dialogue and narrative is achieved, a sequence of things can be accomplished. The proper blend allows the writer to:

1. Create an environment or a culture through the use of dialect, slang or idiom.
2. Provide the reader with all the necessary factual background needed to understand the characters or conflicts that exist at the opening of the narrative.
3. Demonstrate how the words of the characters, as they interact with one another, might support or counterpoint their inner thoughts, feelings and ambitions.
4. Develop, compound and intensify the basic conflict through realistic verbal interchange among characters.

Setting the Tone

The creation of a totally alien environment or culture is common practice among science fiction writers. Many times, the writer will take his plot and place it on a different planet, perhaps at a time in the future. The language or idiom used by the characters should both inform the reader about the place and the people and pinpoint the time as perhaps that of the future.

In her philosophical novella, *Anthem,* Ayn Rand has her characters speak to one another in the first person plural. In effect, the characters are constantly employing a "royal we." This sets the tone of a culture where the word "I" as well as the individualism it connotes are forbidden. As the story develops, she allows one character, her protagonist, to utter the forbidden word and break away from the repressive, collectivist culture. The idiom of the characters sets up the conflict.

Robert Heinlein, long considered the dean of American science fiction writers, uses dialogue early in many of his stories to set the place, time and tone of the work. A good example can be seen in his short story, "Space Jockey."

> Just as they were leaving the telephone called his name. "Don't answer it," she pleaded. "We'll miss the curtain."
>
> "Who is it," he called out. The viewplate lighted; he recognized Olga Pierce and behind her the Colorado Springs office of Trans-Lunar Transit.
>
> "Calling Mister Pemberton. Calling — Oh, it's you, Jake. You're on. Flight 27, Supra New York to Space Terminal. I'll have a copter pick you up in 20 minutes."
>
> "How come?" he protested. "I'm fourth down on the call board."
>
> "You *were* fourth down. Now you are stand-by pilot to Hicks — and he just got a psycho down-check."
>
> "Hicks got psyched? That's silly!"
>
> "Happens to the best, chum. Be ready. Bye, now."

In the first dozen or so lines, we can see that the protagonist, Pemberton, is a pilot of a space vessel sometime in Earth's future. We know that flights to the moon are regular happenings and that he is about to pilot a flight. We also know that some pilots have received "Psych" damage from their jobs and that Jake Pemberton does not relish having his free time taken from him by a mission. There is efficiency in the culture that Heinlein creates as well as a casual quality to interpersonal communication. The characters do not take any special notice of the notion of a "Supra New York to Space Terminal" jaunt and the reader is thus cued to take the same attitude.

Heinlein does much the same thing in his novel, *The Moon Is a Harsh Mistress.* We are immediately introduced to a protagonist-narrator named Manuel Garcia O'Kelly. "Manny" speaks to us and a friendly computer named "Mike" in a terse, yet interesting Russian accent. In a matter of a few pages, the dialogue tells us that Manny represents at least four nationalities; that he is a technician for hire on the moon and that the time is 2075. Manny's name and accent are central to the plot, as the other "loonies" tend to share his cosmopolitan heritage.

Perhaps the best example of Heinlein's setting the tone of a culture in dialogue can be seen in his novella " 'If This Goes On . . .'." The narrator gives us first person exposition in a reasonably contemporary idiom. However, the first dialogue that appears shatters that easy, comfortable style.

"Peace be unto you, Sister."

She had jumped and then suppressed a squeal, then had gathered her dignity to answer. "And to you, little brother."

It was then that I had seen on her forehead the seal of Solomon, the mark of the personal family of the Prophet. "Your pardon, Elder Sister. I did not see. . . . Do you attend the Holy One this night, Elder Sister?"

It is clear from the formal tone of the dialogue that the

culture places a high value on ceremony, ritual and rank. As the rest of the story unfolds, the reader sees that the country is in the grip of a religious dictatorship. Again, the dialogue has set the tone for the culture and the conflict that is to grip it.

Of Conflict and Character

The second opportunity that dialogue provides is to give the reader sufficient background on the characters and conflicts that he or she can proceed without the need for lengthy expository passages. Breaking the flow of action for a passage of formal exposition jolts the reader and breaks concentration. This can hurt when the writer is trying to create suspense or mystery.

A good technique for creating exposition through dialogue was invented by French playwrights of the nineteenth century. The "Well Made Play" was written almost by formula. The first scene of the play provided all of the exposition that the audience would need to understand the beginning conflict as it started to unfold. Dramatists have dubbed this obligatory first scene "The Featherduster Scene." In general terms, the scene progresses like this:

The servants of the middle-class home enter the drawing room and start to clean it. As they clean, they gossip about the things that have taken place in the house recently. The prime topic of conversation is the master of the house and his activities or the mistress and hers. Perhaps the butler tells the maid that the lady of the house returned unexpectedly from a visit to relatives in another city, the night before. He says that she caught her husband in an embarrassing situation with the housekeeper. The maid begs for details and the butler tells her that the lady of the house has fired the housekeeper and is threatening to leave her husband. Both of them plod through the rest of the scene, worrying that they might lose their jobs.

At the end of the scene, one of three characters enters —

the husband, wife or housekeeper. At the moment of that entrance, we know about that character and the immediate crisis he or she is facing. In the ensuing scenes, the other characters of the triangle enter and interact. Additional characters may be introduced as the play progresses. But we are given all of the exposition we need for the major characters before the first one has set foot on the stage.

I don't mean to suggest that the novice contrive a scene to happen. Nor should all stories start with immediate expository dialogue. The basic idea is simply to get across what is necessary to the plot and characters early in the story, so that you don't have to interrupt or backtrack to do it at a later date. Dialogue is a clear, interesting, unobtrusive way to do this.

On occasion, the principal characters can be discussing something themselves at the beginning of the story. The nature of the characters and the conflict should become apparent very quickly. If the writer takes more than a few pages to develop this initial dialogue, there is a chance that the reader will get confused, disinterested or downright bored.

A good example of dialogue's serving to set up conflict and character background can be seen in a later passage from Heinlein's "Space Jockey."

In the passage quoted earlier, the identity of the hero (Jake Pemberton), his profession, the future setting and technology have all been set in a few lines of dialogue. Jake has been called to his job earlier than anticipated. In the subsequent lines with his wife, the major conflict of the story becomes clear.

> His wife was twisting 16 dollars worth of lace handkerchief into a shapeless mass. "Jake, this is ridiculous. For three months I haven't seen enough of you to know what you look like."
>
> "Sorry, kid. Take Helen to the show."

"Oh, Jake, I don't care about the show; I wanted to get you where they couldn't get you for once."
"They would have called me at the theater."
"Oh, no! I wiped out the record you'd left."
"Phyllis! Are you trying to get me fired?"
"Don't look at me that way."

With this brief exchange, there's almost no question as to what the nature of the conflict will be. Add to it the previous segment of dialogue between Jake and Olga Pierce from "Trans-Lunar Transit" and the picture is complete.

Counterpoint

A third possible use of dialogue is to set up counterpoint, or counter-conflict. If you're writing a story in which the thoughts of the characters are available to the reader (a third person story, sometimes called "omniscient"), it's possible to alternate dialogue and thoughts in such a way that several different sets of internal and external conflicts are created.

Assume you've created a character named Adams. Through his thoughts, we see that he hates his boss, a character named Brown. Adams's thoughts tell us that he's finally fed up with Brown. He's tired of working for the man and taking orders and he's going to kill Brown with his bare hands as soon as Brown arrives. With this information, we build up expectations of mayhem and violence. There's no question in the mind of the reader at this point that Adams is a man of action; a rash man; a violent man who will stop at nothing until he wreaks revenge on Brown.

You switch the scene to the outside hall, where Brown is about to enter. Through revealing his thoughts, the reader is made to see that Brown also dislikes Adams. He has little use for the man and would fire him in a minute if he wasn't essential to the job or project that Brown heads. Brown pushes open the door and enters the room where Adams is waiting for him. You shift the two men into dialogue.

> Brown's eyes caught those of Adams as the door swung
> inward. He looked at his subordinate and smiled.
> "Hi, Able! Good to see you. How've you been?" Adams
> paused and then forced a smile.
> "Fine, Brown. Been fine. Hope you had a good week-
> end?"

Suddenly, everything is changed. Adams is not the blood-
thirsty, rash man of action that we thought him to be when
we were exposed to his thoughts. The dialogue has reversed
a set of expectations. Adams looks like a coward, a blowhard,
a hypocrite. Brown, for whom there was no reversal, seems
the more diplomatic of the two. He knows that he has to
keep Adams on the job, and he is trying, through tact, to
do it.

If we altered the situation a bit and had Brown think what
a wonderful worker Adams was and how much he liked him
as a person, we would, through the ensuing dialogue, paint
Adams as a dangerous man, perhaps even a psychotic.

The conflicts demonstrated by the brief sequence are:

1. Adams's hatred of Brown versus his inability to
express it.
2. Brown's dislike of Adams versus his need for the
man as a worker.
3. Brown's concern that Adams not see the dislike.
4. Adams's friendly pose that seems to demonstrate
the same concern.

It's possible to compound the conflict even more by bringing
other persons into the room. Perhaps the characters could
be placed at a party, where it is necessary that they not show
any of their mutual resentment to each other or any other
guests.

Perhaps the two characters could be thrown together on

a desert island, or asteroid, or spaceship, where that resentment could be allowed to grow, until it blossomed into violence at a crucial point — say, where one man had to help the other. There are hundreds of possible permutations that could be made to grow out of such a situation where the thoughts of the characters counter their dialogue.

Escalating the Conflict

The final use of dialogue that I've listed — though it's clearly not the final one possible — is to develop, compound and intensify the basic conflict of your story through dialogue between the characters. In essence, let the characters fight out their dispute in dialogue. Mix the dialogue with any other narrated form of conflict you wish.

An excellent example of this head-to-head confrontation in science fiction can be seen in William Jon Watkins's excellent novel, *CLICKWHISTLE.* In the following sequence, Admiral Flushing, commander of the nuclear sub Dolphin Four, is assigned to brief Councilman Stuart, a government inspector, on the operation of the ship. The Admiral resents the intrusion of the inspector. The inspector resents the Navy in general. Note the way the narrative comments that either precede or follow each of the characters' statements intensify the conflict.

> Stuart turned again. "Isn't two missiles rather light armament for half the Atlantic fleet?"
>
> Flushing forced another smile. "We're not exactly half the fleet, Mister Stuart."
>
> Stuart shrugged. "This and Dolphin Three are the only underwater craft with nuclear weapons in the whole Atlantic."
>
> "I'm afraid you overestimate us, Councilman. True, there are only two weapons systems in our class in *this* ocean, but we're only a small part of a much larger system, a sort of seagoing computer terminal."

"Five billion dollars is a high price for a seagoing computer terminal, Admiral," Stuart added without a smile.

"An expensive but necessary deterrent," the Admiral countered.

"Two multiple warhead missiles don't sound like much of a deterrent."

There's little question that the men are taking every opportunity to rip at one another. The question arises, "How does one end such an interchange?" Watkins adds the complication of a problem with one of the missiles. It is this factor that diverts the men to another problem without lessening their distaste for one another. The diversion from this conflict is the mechanical voice of a computer. It is set off from the dialogue of the two men by appearing in upper case letters.

DISARMING CREW REPORTS HATCH WILL NOT RESPOND TO MECHANICAL OVERRIDE."
Flushing cut in. "Then try manu . . . ."
"MANUAL OVERRIDE NEGATIVE FUNCTION. BLAST DOOR ALSO NEGATIVE FUNCTION."
"Then get a torch down there and cut it open."
"SECONDARY CREW SENT FOR LASER TORCH. APPROXIMATE CUTTING TIME FOR BLAST DOOR ONE HOUR."
"Not the door! Cut through the panel to the control circuits to the right of the door. Cut those circuits! There's only two inches of plastic there. It shouldn't take more than 15 minutes there."
"APPROXIMATE CUTTING TIME FOURTEEN MINUTES."
Flushing groaned. "Get another torch."
"CREW DISPATCHED FOR SECOND TORCH. CUTTING TIME APPROXIMATELY EIGHT MIN-

UTES. MISSILE HATCH STILL OPENED. MISSILE
STILL ARMED."

"Where is it aimed? Maybe we can fire it."

"PRESENT SETTING ZERO DEGREES. DIRECT-
LY OVERHEAD. STRATOSPHERIC DETONATION
POSSIBLE WITHOUT DAMAGE TO SATELLITES
OF EITHER "SEAPACT" OR "EASTHEM" NA-
TIONS, IF LAUNCH IS CARRIED OUT IN WITHIN
TEN MINUTES."

Flushing shouted. "Deactivation crew! Keep cutting!"

While it is clear that the conflict between Flushing and
Stuart has been overwhelmed, the discussion between Flushing and the computer is equally frustrating. The dialogue
exchange is used to heighten the tension of the moment in
a way that a simple narrative could not. This then is a direct
conflict between characters or forces, built on a fabric of clear
dialogue.

Getting Underway

A few of the uses and purposes of dialogue have been
made clear. Now — how do we get started? Getting past the
first line of anything is a large job for many writers. In fact,
many writers do the first chapter after the rest of the book
has been written. Many skip whole chapters that might slow
them down, and complete these only after the balance of
the book has been completed. This can be done only if a
good outline for the work in progress is in hand.

One of the best axioms to follow in the creation of dialogue
is: "The words are only as meaningful as the characters that
speak them." In essence, the dialogue is as good as the
character development for the speakers. Developing characters in advance can help considerably. Try to sketch out on
paper or in your mind those characteristics that make up
your character. Ask yourself some questions.

What part of the country is the character from?

What level of education does the character have?

What does the character do for a living?

What are the character's emotions like?

If you can create answers for these questions, as well as other questions you might like to devise, there is a good chance that the character's dialogue will ring true for the reader. For example, if the character is from Maine, a little regional twang in his or her voice might add to believability. If the character has a reasonably high level of education, there's reason to assume that he or she might have precise, clipped speech, with a minimum of slang. The questions and answers can go on for as long as it takes to get a "real" sound to the character's speech.

If you have trouble phrasing the speech of a character, it might not be a bad idea to sit among strangers and just listen to their speech patterns. Perhaps you could listen to a conversation and then try to duplicate it on paper as you heard it. This can be facilitated by a small tape recorder. Transcribe what you have heard. Get a feel for how it looks on paper.

The next step in the creation of meaningful dialogue is the development of what many writers call "stage directions." These are the indicators that slide the conversation back and forth between characters. The beginning dialogue writer will often find himself in a deadly dull Ping-Pong match of "he said ... she said ... he said ... she said." The first step in overcoming this is that mentioned earlier. Find a distinctive speech pattern for your character(s). With clear, distinctive patterns, the reader will never have to ask which character is speaking. If there are two characters speaking, simple quotes around their lines — with no stage directions at all — is possible over short stretches.

A good set of stage directions can be seen in the *CLICK-WHISTLE* segment quoted earlier. If you review the dialogue, you will see that there isn't one "he said" in the entire sequence. Stage directions that indicate movement, mood or tone are all stated in synonyms. You might buy a good dictionary of synonyms that could help build this capacity.

Yet another part of dialogue development is the use of reactions. There are times when it isn't appropriate for characters to react in sentences or even phrases. Sometimes they might simply have to emit sounds. Grunts, whistles, groans, screams and hiccups can all be used in lieu of fully articulated reactions. The best of these can be created by phonetically recreating the sound. There are some standard reactions that are generally accepted by readers. "A..hem!" "Phew!" These are onomatopoeia: the exact duplications of sounds in print.

When sound replication fails or gets boring, several writers have employed print conventions in their place. For example, a writer in my acquaintance has stopped using words like "Wha...?" when he wants to express surprise or disbelief. He simply uses "?" It serves the purpose.

Lastly, a good convention to remember, when dialogue will be interspersed with narrative and stage directions, is to use a new paragraph for each new speaker. Check your own reading and you will see that generally you automatically take new paragraphs to denote new speakers.

Consider this as you weigh the value of dialogue. The average Twentieth Century novel that has had any degree of success is composed of over 30 and perhaps as much as 50 percent dialogue. So, don't just describe. Demonstrate! Use dialogue!

The foundation upon which a solid story rests is, of course, the plot and the idea behind the plot. Without this combination, the new writer very often finds himself creating vignettes and isolated scenes rather than a forward-moving short story. This, too, is something that today's editor finds himself besieged with — and though the writing may be fine, even excellent, if it is not a story, he will not buy it.

This article explores both ends of this plot-idea foundation with an eye toward guiding the new writer toward a sale rather than a rejection slip.

James Gunn, *an instructor of English at the University of Kansas, is one of SF's long-time revered authors. His many stories and novels, his term as Past President of SFWA, and his several nonfiction articles and books have given him one of the largest followings among readers and fans in the field.*

CHAPTER 4:

Where Do You Get Those Crazy Ideas?

by
James Gunn

Science fiction is often called a literature of ideas. No one should be surprised, then, to learn that the most important part of writing a science fiction story is getting a good idea; and that the question laymen always ask science fiction writers is, "Where do you get those crazy ideas?"

That's us — the people with the crazy ideas. It's no use saying, "You mean crazy ideas like atomic energy, space travel, overpopulation, pollution, automation, catastrophes, holocausts, technological change, evolution, and all the other limitless possibilities in a universe which may be infinite and possibly eternal?" It doesn't even do any good to ask, "How can you keep from having crazy ideas when you are living in a world that is changing while you look at it? How can you avoid wondering what will happen next when life is one surprise after another? How can you avoid speculating about the direction change is heading and where it will take us and how this will affect the way people live and feel and behave?"

So I just shrug and say, "Oh, crazy ideas come easy when you're in the business."

This business — crazy ideas — has become the last frontier of the short story writer. Anyone who wants to begin writing by selling short stories, which is much the easiest way to begin, had better try to write science fiction, because that's about the only market left. There may be about three detective magazines still, but the biggest market for short fiction in this country still is the half dozen or so science fiction magazines and the ten to 20 or more original science fiction anthologies. And the market for noncategory stories exists mainly in the little magazines which pay little or nothing.

Even in the field of the novel, science fiction has passed the western and is creeping up on the mystery.

Moreover, science fiction always has been peculiarly receptive to the beginning writer.

Write 'Em Down — Fast

If people persist in asking where I get my crazy ideas, I usually dig deeper into what some authorities call creativity and what I call habit. Noticing the fictional possibilities in the information that flows into my head has become a pattern of behavior: "What a great idea for a story!"

Ideas, of course, are not unique to science fiction. Every story, of any kind, demands an idea, though it may be less specific, less speculative. Students in my fiction writing classes with some writing experience generalize their complaint. "I can't come up with anything to write about," they say. That's another way of asking, "How do you get an idea?"

That's such a preposterous complaint that I usually begin by saying to them the same thing I say to the laymen: "How do you avoid getting ideas?" I have card files stuffed with ideas for stories, and desk drawers jammed with story ideas jotted down on odd scraps of paper. I'll never have time to get to all of them, not even to ten percent of them. The problem of every real writer is not getting ideas but finding the time to write.

I admit that this answer is a bit unfair. It wasn't always this way with me. I tell my students about the second time I turned to freelance writing. It was more serious this time: now I had a wife and a child; I wasn't experimenting but trying to make a career of it. I returned from a trip to New York City where I had been talking to editors; I had a couple of story ideas and a panicky feeling that I might never have another. That was the moment when I began jotting down every idea that occurred to me. Soon I had a stack of them and I never panicked again. About that.

That leads me to a point I should make early: write ideas down. A few words are enough. The idea that comes to you at an odd moment, as you are reading or watching something happen outside your window or listening to a lecture or laying awake in bed at night or dreaming, the idea that seems so magnificent and unforgettable, will vanish within hours, even minutes, never to be recalled – unless it is written down. All of them will not seem as wonderful when reread; many golden ideas turn into lead with the passage of time; but some will retain that magic ability to recreate excitement every time the author touches them. Those are the ones with the basic quality every idea for fiction should have: of impelling the writer toward the typewriter to turn them into story. Excitement, a glow in the stomach, a fire in the head – that's how a writer recognizes a good idea.

On Speculation

But where does he get the idea in the first place? Since he is a writer, he reads – no one who isn't in love with reading should consider writing as a career or even an avocation – and he gets ideas as he reads. It doesn't matter whether it is fiction or nonfiction, a newspaper, a magazine or a book.

In science fiction, speculation about new developments in the hard or soft sciences is the source of many story concepts. Once this kind of speculation was more prevalent in the general magazines such as *Scientific American, Time, Newsweek, Saturday Review,* or *Psychology Today;* the scientific journals were likely to leave the speculation to others. This is changing as science becomes more aware of its responsibilities and more willing to consider the consequences of its discoveries. An experienced science fiction writer can build his own speculative world on a bare description of some discovery, but most of us can benefit from the informed projections of other, more experienced minds.

Once scientists were not much good at speculation. To know too much about a subject inhibits the ability to think wild thoughts. But recent discoveries have shaken up the conservatives who used to feel that they knew not only most of what was known but at least the general nature of what could be known about their disciplines. New and unexpected breakthroughs in astronomy and physics, chemistry, biology and other sciences have loosened the chains of reality that bound the scientific imagination. Today the craziest ideas are being thought by astrophysicists such as Carl Sagan and Freeman Dyson.

Larry Niven got the basic idea for *Ringworld* from speculations by Dyson that a truly advanced civilization would be able to use all the energy radiated by its sun; it would be able to reconstruct the planets of that sun into a sphere completely enclosing the sun. The inhabitants would live on the inside of the sphere and not only enjoy all of the sun's energy but a vastly increased living area. Dyson's point was that such civilizations would be invisible in the visual spectrum, but would radiate the sun's energy as heat in the infrared; thus we might be able to detect advanced civilizations by picking up strong infrared where we could see no star.

The concept of the gigantic living space captured Niven's imagination. He changed it, however, into a gigantic ring — a slice from Dyson's sphere — a million miles wide and encircling the sun.

My novel *The Listeners* was inspired by reading Walter Sullivan's *We Are Not Alone,* a historical survey of efforts to communicate with other worlds and an account of speculation by astronomers, beginning in the late fifties, about the possibility of picking up communications from other intelligent creatures in the universe.

Mining Stories From Stories

A writer can even get ideas from encyclopedias, almanacs or statistical reports. I was reading an article about "Feeling" in the *Encyclopaedia Britannica;* it developed into an analysis of the various ways to be happy and ended with the final sentence, "But the true science of applied hedonics is not yet born." That statement expanded into my novel *The Joy Makers.*

I got the idea for a fantasy story called "The Beautiful Brew" from a Virgil Partch cartoon that showed two men looking at a mug of beer on which the foam had shaped itself into the bust and head of a girl. The caption was something like: "That guy really puts a head on a glass of beer."

Other people's stories also can be a rich source of ideas. The first few paragraphs of a popular story are intended to intrigue the reader, to draw him into the story; in addition they suggest what the story is going to be about, and in the best-crafted stories they *tell* the reader what is going to happen, how the story is going to end, but in such a way the reader doesn't understand. Often then, after reading the first few paragraphs of a story, I find myself thinking ahead; sometimes I'm wrong about how the story will develop, but then I have a story idea of my own.

Or, as it often happens in science fiction, the reader may find himself disagreeing with the author's solution to a basic concept and use the author's situation to reach a different resolution, sometimes exactly the opposite, as Robert Heinlein's *Starship Troopers* inspired Gordon Dickson to write *Naked to the Stars,* and Harry Harrison, *Bill, the Galactic Hero.*

Or the writer may take the emotional impact of a story and translate that into other situations, as I tried to do with the ending of Graham Greene's *The Heart of the Matter* in an otherwise totally dissimilar story called "The Power and the Glory."

Firsthand Experience — First-Rate Source for Ideas

Sometimes a writer may approach the problem of idea from the angle of story, that is, from the interrelationships of people. A human problem often can be intensified in a science fiction situation, or it can be considered more dispassionately in a cooler environment than our hot contemporary scene with all of its instant preconceptions and prejudices.

Thus a story of lovers may achieve new levels of emotion if they are separated by time rather than distance, as in Heinlein's *The Door Into Summer;* or if one is a human being and the other is an android, as in Lester del Rey's "Helen O'Loy" or J. T. McIntosh's "Made in U.S.A." The generation gap may become more significant if parents are discovered plotting against their children, as in my story "The Old Folks," or if the son is a superman, as in Henry Kuttner's "Absalom"; and the problems of parenthood can be dramatized more effectively if the infant is an omnipotent superman, as in Kuttner's "When the Bough Breaks."

Possibilities such as these can occur to a writer while he is reading other kinds of literature, or while glancing over the feature and human interest stories in the day's newspaper. Such capsule stories about real human beings suggest to the writer what he can never satisfactorily invent: the fantastic variety of situations into which men and women can involve themselves, and the fantastic variety in which men and women exist.

Finally, the writer can get ideas from observation — by watching people, by listening to conversations, by absorbing the anecdotes of friends or relations . . . . Or, best of all, from personal experience, which is the writer's unique source of inspiration. It is all he ever has in the end, even in science fiction. One of my best-known stories, "The Misogynist," was based on my own experience with women. On an index card one day in 1950, I jotted down, "Women are aliens." Six months later, when I had come up with a viewpoint character and a way of handling the narration, I had a unique story.

A Twist on the Future

Science fiction has a great deal of concept sharing. It is a close community of writers, even of readers, and one writer will construct his story on another writer's premises or extrapolations. "Science fiction builds upon science fiction," Donald Wollheim wrote in his personal history of science fiction, *The Universe Makers.* Simply rewriting an old idea is worse than nothing; a writer must bring to his story some new vision, some different twist, which will reinvigorate the concept. Science fiction demands novelty; that is both its distinction for the reader and its problem for the writer.

Novelty is not always easy. In my illustrated history of science fiction, *Alternate Worlds,* I encompass all of the themes of science fiction in 14 phrases: 1) far traveling; 2) the wonders of science; 3) man and the machine; 4) progress; 5) man and his society; 6) man and the future; 7) war; 8) cataclysm; 9) man and his environment; 10) superpowers; 11) superman; 12) man and alien; 13) man and religion; and 14) miscellaneous glimpses of the future or the past. Within these broad categories, however, lie an infinity of unique perceptions about man and his racial possibilities.

Science fiction is "origin of species fiction," wrote English critic Edmund Crispin, and almost all of the concepts of science fiction have racial implications. Trivial topics have little success. Novelty and meaning, meaning and novelty — a new idea, a different perspective, significance. . . . The demands that science fiction makes on writers drains them, sometimes drives them into writer's blocks.

And yet a writer who is good enough can pick up an old idea and make it as good as new. Heinlein did that with a 1951 novel called *The Puppet Masters,* which took the old theme of invasion by alien monsters, made them parasites, and created an effective new story. In his collection of novellas, *Born with the Dead,* Robert Silverberg made brilliant new use of three old ideas: the revivification of the dead, the sun stopped in the heavens, and euthanasia.

Get Fresh

Originality, however, is safest for the beginning writer. If he should be so incautious or so unaware as to submit a story about flying saucers, visitors from other worlds who turn out to be our ancestors, World War III, or even time travel, he is likely to receive in the return mail only a printed rejection slip, or at best a note reading, "Heinlein did it better." Young writers naturally begin with imitation; they get turned toward writing because they love reading and admire the work of particular writers. But the novice must break with the past; he must do his own thing rather than pale or inept reworkings. The new writer is wise to avoid ideas that end with classic revelations: the alien castaways on Earth who turn out to be Adam and Eve, the catastrophe that turns out to have destroyed Atlantis, the character sent to Earth (or out of the future) to save it from destruction who turns out to be Christ or Mohammed or Buddha. . . . David Gerrold wrote *The Man Who Folded Himself,* Michael Moorcock wrote *Behold the Man,* and most of us have tried our hand at old themes and done them badly or well, but the beginning writer should leave that practice for his more experienced, later incarnation. Harlan Ellison could take the old theme of the omnipotent computer that rebels against its human masters, that becomes a tyrannical God, and make it new again in "I Have No Mouth and I Must Scream"; that is no job for a novice.

The beginning writer should try to find a new perception. John Campbell, the late, long-time editor of the magazine that was born as *Astounding* and became *Analog,* said 20 years ago: "The reader wants the author to do one of two basic things — and prefers the author who does both. The author's function is to imagine for the reader, of course — but he must either (a) imagine in greater detail than the reader has, or (b) imagine something the reader hasn't thought of. Ideally, the author imagines something new, in greater detail."

Get a fresh idea. That demands a considerable familiarity with science fiction, of course, in order to identify what has been done before. A good place to start is the *Science Fiction Hall of Fame,* Volumes I and II, but there are other good anthologies. A hopeful writer of science fiction should have read everything he could find — short stories, novels, magazines, books. . . . Then he may be ready to distinguish the old from the new, the bad from the good.

Detail Work

Once the writer has a fresh idea, he should explore its implications; he should imagine it in depth, the way Hal Clement imagined the "whirligig world" of extremely high gravity where his *Mission of Gravity* took place; or Frederik Pohl and Cyril Kornbluth imagined the world controlled by advertising agencies that they created in *The Space Merchants.* Then the writer must imagine people trapped in that world, up against things, forced to do things they don't want to do or can't do, trying to adjust or trying to change the conditions.

In Tom Godwin's touchstone story "The Cold Equations," the pilot of an emergency delivery ship is forced to eject an innocent girl stowaway into airless space because otherwise the ship would crash and its essential cargo be lost. Where did he get that crazy idea? Perhaps by considering the traditional story in which women and children are saved first, no matter what the cost.

In John W. Campbell's novelet "Who Goes There?" a group of Antarctic scientists discover buried deep in the ice an alien monster that has the power to absorb any protoplasm and imitate it perfectly. Where did Campbell get the idea? He had written "The Brain Stealers of Mars" a few years before; it concerned the ability of Martian creatures to read minds and turn themselves into confusing duplicates. Campbell returned to the idea in "Who Goes There?" with a different setting and one small alteration: the imitated protoplasm must first be eaten.

Robert Heinlein's "Universe" begins with the idea of a spaceship which is a world in itself. Murray Leinster had described one in his "Proxima Centauri," but Heinlein added the facts that the ship must travel for generations to reach its goal and that a mutiny had destroyed awareness of mission and meaning until the survivors consider the ship to be the entire universe and their remembered history as parable.

In "A Martian Odyssey" Stanley Weinbaum asked whether aliens had to be unfriendly, and if an intelligent alien could not learn to communicate quickly with a reasonably intelligent human.

We know where Isaac Asimov got the idea for "Nightfall," the classic story in which a world is surrounded by six suns and a moon so that night falls only once every 2,050 years, at which time the inhabitants of that world go mad and burn their civilizations to make light. John Campbell challenged Asimov with a quotation from Emerson (Asimov used it as an epigraph to his story): "If the stars should appear one night in a thousand years, how would men believe and adore, and preserve for many generations the remembrance of the city of God!"

Murray Leinster took the old idea of "First Contact" with

aliens and pointed out that it need not be a deadly encounter, no matter how much is at stake, even racial survival, if a trade-off can be conceived that is more profitable than conflict.

We might speculate that Arthur Clarke got the idea for "The Nine Billion Names of God" when he learned that Tibetan monks are trying to enumerate all the names of God as they spin their prayer wheels; when they have done so, the world will end. In Clarke's story they obtain a computer to do the job in 100 days instead of 15,000 years.

In 1941 Lester del Rey asked himself what would happen if something went wrong in an atomic factory; his answer was "Nerves." Cyril Kornbluth noted in 1951 that successful people were limiting their families, and unsuccessful people were not; he foresaw "The Marching Morons." In 1947 Jack Williamson wondered what a perfect machine would do to humanity, and visualized it doing everything so much better that mankind was left "With Folded Hands."

Horace Gold, founding editor of *Galaxy,* suggested to Fred Pohl that the problems of poverty might some day be supplanted by the problems of affluence; if you were poor you would have to consume more, and if you were rich you could afford to live simply. When Pohl solved the fictional problems, he wrote "The Midas Plague."

Character Under Stress

Not all stories can be reduced to this kind of simple summary, just as not all ideas can be traced to a single source. Many stories are either more complex or dependent upon mood or description or style. But somewhere there is an idea lurking behind the finished product, even if it is only an idea for a setting where something important or exciting must happen, or a character to whom something must happen, or a situation that places a character under stress.

Fiction, John Ciardi once said, is character under stress.

It doesn't matter whether you start with the character and develop the stress that will peculiarly test that character, or if you start with the stress and invent a character who will be peculiarly tested by it. My own definition of a short story is: "a short piece of prose narrative about a human problem which is complicated by events and resolved satisfactorily." The problem must be *human,* or, in stories with protagonists who are animals or aliens, problems that we can imagine as human, with which we can identify; otherwise readers are uninvolved and uninterested. There must be a *problem,* or it is only a sketch or a description or an essay; to use the term "short story" for slice-of-life pieces only confuses matters, for then we must find another name for the narrative in which a problem occurs that a protagonist must solve; moreover the two kinds of writing have different impacts upon the reader. The problem must be *complicated* — made more difficult, more urgent — and by *events,* not just reflection, because this process intensifies our concern about the person with the problem and builds up to a final payoff of satisfaction. The problem must be *resolved,* or we feel that the writer has promised us something he did not deliver; and it must be resolved *satisfactorily* — that is, the problem posed must be the one resolved, and the resolution must satisfy the promises the rest of the story has made.

The beginning writer will start with no idea, no problem, no sympathetic character; the events of his narrative will be haphazard rather than directed at complicating the story's problem, if there are any events; and if he has a resolution, it will not resolve the problem posed, or it will resolve it in a way that is cheap, easy, or out of character.

Acting It Out

How, then, does the beginning writer recognize a good idea when it comes to him? First of all by its originality, second by the excitement it engenders in him to get to a typewriter, third by its ability to attract good characters, to collect places where the idea must happen, to lead somewhere, to put characters under stress, to force characters to act, and finally to resolve itself.

A good idea becomes good fiction when it states itself in terms of human conflict; up to that time it is merely an interesting observation, such as "women are aliens," or "the advertising agencies are taking over the world," or "only persons willing to perform military service should be permitted to vote."

A person with a file drawer full of good ideas is not yet a writer; he must turn those ideas into stories. That requires some uncommon attributes. We hear, for instance, that writers are sensitive. Some are; some aren't. But every good writer is conscious of sensory stimuli. He is visually alert and aware of sounds and smells and tastes and the feel of things. He puts these things into his stories, when they are appropriate, when he is striving for verisimilitude, because he knows that no place exists in reality or in fiction without appearance, without sound and smell — and some cannot exist without taste or feel.

In addition, the writer must have certain skills, not only in the use of words but in the techniques of fiction. He should know the difference between summary and drama, what Carolyn Gordon and Allen Tate call the panorama and the scene. Panorama is the broad view generally encountered in a summary of events or in exposition; it is sometimes necessary but usually nondramatic. Scene is the closeup; it shows things happening before the reader's eyes; it is drama, and everything else is only preparation for it. Often the beginning writer summarizes everything, and ends up with a scenario. The experienced writer visualizes the action of the story happening in front of him like a stage play, and reports it to the reader as it happens. He writes in scenes; as Henry James urged, he doesn't tell — he shows.

The writer gets involved. Harlan Ellison says that when he is writing a story he paces around and acts out all the parts. I find myself gesturing and speaking bits of dialogue. Anyone passing by must think us strange indeed.

Take Care With Your Characters

It helps a beginning writer to see the story's action as a struggle between a sympathetic character and his or her opposition, whether it is another character or a natural obstacle or conditions. Usually a character must accomplish something or take an action that is important to him. His coping, or being unable to cope, with the situation is what creates reader interest; the sophistication of the story emerges through the ingenuity of the situation, the cleverness of the resolution, the verisimilitude of the details, the subtlety of the presentation, the appropriateness and the wit of the language, and the validity of the observations of life and character.

I stress sympathy in character because too many beginning writers present characters who are at best passive and at worst unlikable or incompetent or uncaring or dull; we cannot become interested in them because we know from the beginning that they don't want anything we want, or if they do then they won't get it and the resolution will be obvious or omitted or invalid. I don't mean, of course, that they must be "nice" people or even "good" people; but they must be people whose problems we can imagine being involved in, no matter how outlandish, and whose responses to those problems we can understand. We can even use a character we dislike, whom we want to see fail, but he must be threatening someone we care about.

I also stress the importance of the action the character must take. Too often beginning writers set a task that is unimportant, often easily accomplished, for the characters; they don't care much about it, and the reader cares nothing at all.

Honor Thy Contract

Reader involvement is the only way to create a successful story. The writer establishes an implicit contract with every person he can induce to read his story: you invest your money and your time, and I will entertain you in a certain way; I will show you a person whose situation will intrigue you, and I will show you that person coping or failing to cope with that problem in a way that will provide you with a pleasant suspense and a final satisfaction that is your reward for reading.

One reason fiction has been dying is that too many readers have been disappointed too often. They have become disillusioned by broken contracts.

All of this doesn't mean formula writing; or it means formula only insofar as life itself is a formula. Our main business in life is success, however we measure it; sometimes success is just survival, sometimes getting what we want or love and avoiding what we dislike or hate; sometimes it is finding what is important and real in life. But it all begins with birth and progresses through various stages until death ends it, and the various combinations are limited in broad outline. They move naturally — in a formula, if you will — through growing up, into adulthood and responsibility, to independence and the effort to get an appropriate share of the world's goods, to romance and the problems with love that does not endure, to the deterioration of the body and the mind which extends through middle age into senility. In between we have various subthemes such as the difficulties of communication, the search for meaning, and the battle between tradition and change. A formula is something that, like human experience, is infinitely repeated.

Heinlein has said that there are only three basic plots: 1) boy meets girl, the romance; 2) the little tailor, the character who must solve a problem; 3) the person who learns better, the character who believes one thing about himself or his world and learns that he has been wrong.

Plots can be sliced in other ways, depending upon the element one chooses to emphasize. One is the story of the child developing into an adult, the rite of passage; another, the revelation of the true nature of life or oneself, the story of sudden truth. And most stories involve several plot types: a romance within a problem story, for instance, and possibly the man who learns better as well.

What distinguishes a story from a sketch is that in a story something changes. Usually someone changes; but sometimes it is only his circumstances, as in the case of many adventure heroes — Conan or James Bond or Kimball Kinnison. But even in the most adventurous of stories, usually the protagonist has been changed by his experience, if only to the extent of satisfying, for the moment, his desire for adventure.

Checklist

Final recommendations for the beginning writer:

1. Begin with a worthwhile idea, preferably one that is fresh and new, but at least one that hasn't been exhausted.

2. Create characters who can ideally dramatize your idea. Make them suffer; make their suffering move them to action.

3. Plan out a scheme of action — a plot — that will present all the scenes necessary to show the characters working out their problem(s).

4. Omit everything that doesn't advance the plot — unnecessary scenes or casual conversation or pointless characters. Everything must work; everything must con-

tribute. Ask yourself: if I leave this out, will it matter? If the answer is no, leave it out. Like a sculptor who creates a statue out of a block of stone by chipping away everything that isn't statue, remove everything from what you have written that isn't story.

5. Start your story in the middle of things, as Homer began the *Iliad.* This is the point where the problem of the story is stated; where characters are show in the grip of the situation. Then, if you must, backtrack to exposition. Exposition is dead material, however, and is best integrated into the action of the story.

6. Avoid clichés in plot, characterization and phrasing. This is difficult for the beginning writer, because every writer begins as a reader in love with someone else's ideas. Learning to avoid the trite is half the task of learning to write.

7. Write in scenes; visualize them completely; bring in other sensory detail when possible.

8. Dramatize everything you can; try to eliminate everything that isn't dramatic.

9. Revise.

10. Submit what you have written for publication. Heinlein said this a long time ago; it's still true. You must aim at publication.

And if you find a new way to get crazy ideas, please let me know.

One of the trickiest problems in writing science fiction is creating the proper-sounding and proper-meaning terms. Obviously, this entails more than simply throwing together a few syllables minus the consonants or vowels, and certainly more than splicing together a few pseudoscientific terms. This article, then, explores the rights and wrongs of future terminology, shows you a couple of shortcuts and tricks, and explains just why certain terms fail despite their good intentions, and others succeed in spite of themselves.

Poul Anderson *needs no introduction to the SF reader, casual or otherwise. His books and stories have appeared in every major SF and fantasy publication in the world; he is a multiple winner of the Hugo and Nebula Awards, has been a runner-up more times than we can count, and his recent Midsummer Tempest has been nominated as the best novel of the year for the newly-created Lovecraft Award, the first major award given solely for works of fantasy. He is a Past President of SFWA, a member of the Society for Creative Anachronism, and is also a respected writer of mystery fiction.*

CHAPTER 5:

Nomenclature in Science Fiction

by
Poul Anderson

"What's in a name?" asked romantic little Juliet, "that which we call a rose/ By any other name would smell as sweet." But what she was really speaking about was her family and Romeo's. The feud between these would still have existed had Capulets and Montagues possessed different cognomens. And while we would not affect the rose in itself were we to designate it by a harsh sound like "thistle" or "cactus," the fact is that we use a soft, melodious utterance. This may well have influenced us toward thinking of the rose sentimentally, making it a symbol of love and peace, although it is just as prickly as the other two kinds of plant, and they in their own ways are just as beautiful.

The writer who is concerned about his or her craft will early on become aware of the power of names. Humanity has never altogether outgrown word magic. However sophisticated, we are all emotionally affected by qualities like sonority, connotation and association. Good nomenclature will greatly add to the reader's pleasure in a story. Science fiction and, to a lesser extent, fantasy often have an additional use for it: to convey information in the most compact form.

After all, a future society, an alien planet, or any similarly exotic setting must have countless features that do not occur in our twentieth-century terrestrial reality. Some of these must be brought on stage, or the imaginary world will be so sketchy that the reader will justly blame the author for lack of imagination. At the same time, and equally rightly, the reader does not want long, dull discourses on every item commonplace in that world.

Therefore science fiction soon developed a set of words — names — which serve as shorthand for objects (e.g., "spaceship," "spacesuit"), occupations ("spaceman," "coordinator"), pseudoscientific or transscientific ideas ("hyperspace," "android"), social institutions and constructs ("World Federation," "credits" as the units of money), and so on. Several of these are a bit descriptive in themselves, like "blaster," which indicates an energy weapon of some sort, generally a hand gun. A few have become part of language everywhere, like "robot."

By now they are clichés. This is not necessarily bad. Many clichés endure because nobody has ever improved on them: for example, the quotation with which this essay opens, or, to take a single widely used word which, precisely used, still carries tremendous meaning, "chivalrous." Even if a phrasing can be bettered, an author may well choose not to do so, feeling that too many stylistic tricks will unduly clutter his story.

Naturally, freshness is desirable whenever feasible. A new name for an old idea may catch attention. To that end, from my friend the French science fiction writer Francis Carsac, I once borrowed "fulgurator" for "blaster." It did not seem wise, though, to go on and, in English, substitute his "scaphandre" for "spacesuit."

Sometimes a new name may hint at a new idea. For instance, instead of the customary "credit," writers have occasionally expressed the unit of currency as the "pluton," the "rix," the "stellar," or the "golden," to mention just a few. The first and last of these, at least, skillfully employed, can in context reveal something about the economic system of the fictional society. That is, the "credit" may well imply a totally abstract concept of money, such as we are moving toward today, while the "golden" suggests a return to a metallic standard — perhaps because the abstractions have lent themselves too readily to inflation.

Care is always necessary. One author shortened "condominium" to "condom," thereby giving rise to ribald interpretations of his whole text. But Philip K. Dick's "conapt" for more or less the same kind of housing is reasonable, as are such self-explanatory words as "3V" and "vitryl."

Better Explain Zango

Occasionally neologisms can be based on foreign languages. In *The Byworlder* I derived the slang terms "george" for a solid, tax-paying citizen and "sigaroon" for a sort of hobo from the Romany "gorgio" and "Tzigani." The greatest achievement of this sort is doubtless *A Clockwork Orange*, for which Anthony Burgess created a whole vocabulary obviously originating in a period of Russian domination.

Still, throughout most of the world, Greek and Latin roots remain the primary source. They are so well-known that the meaning of a new combination is often plain at first glance, as with the American "astronaut" or the Soviet "cosmonaut." (I must admit to preferring the latter, because it makes more sense to call a spaceman a cosmic voyager than a star voyager. And "astrogator" is a word well lost in obscurity; do airplanes have "aerogators"?)

Hence Greek and Latin are wellsprings of easily understood terms. For instance, a future party of neo-Luddites, who want to destroy all advanced machinery, might well call themselves the Mechanoclasts. While I fear it will never catch on, "eidophone" is infinitely better than "picturephone." L. Sprague de Camp's story title "The Isolinguals" neatly characterizes groups of people each of which has a given language in common, and nothing else. To be sure, the writer must know what he is doing. I forbear to list the terrible malapropisms that mar any number of science fiction stories, including some of the most famous. A Greek and a Latin dictionary, and a little study of the grammars, are a very sound investment.

Granted, many names are not formed on scholarly principles. We don't know the origin of the word "gun," and "gas" was made out of thin air, so to speak. "Tank" was a military code name while armored vehicles running on treads were being developed; it happened to stick, but "pile," which started similarly, has been replaced by "reactor." "Laser" is an acronym. Brand names like "Kleenex" go into general use for whole classes of things. So the science fiction writer can be arbitrary or can violate etymology if he wishes, without sacrificing plausibility. A. E. van Vogt's "beardex" is an ugly word but a believable one with a clear enough meaning, and I have not hesitated to borrow it. However, should I refer to a machine as, say, a "zango," I had better take care that the story context shows what a zango is.

The same principles apply, and become stronger, when we move out from Earth of the fairly near future into distant worlds and times, or the realms of Faerie. In addition, in these more fanciful settings, the need for euphony and for emotional overtones is much greater.

Let us consider the following aspects of an imaginative background: natural environment, geography (including political divisions), sociology and inhabitants. Finally will come a few remarks about constructing a language.

Names For a World

Once, while following an Apollo mission on television, I

heard a commentator solemnly declare that the Moon has no environment. Now actually, as those same missions and the interplanetary flybys and unmanned landings have proven, a world that is lifeless still holds more marvels and mysteries than we can ever guess. Until we can go there to experience them, we rely on our writers to daydream about them for us. Evocative names are part of these dreams.

Any world should at least offer minerals, certain of which may be unlike anything we know on Earth, especially if the strange planet is different in mass, chemical composition, or other physical properties. No doubt men will give rather dull names to most substances, such as "jonesite" for something that somebody called Jones first identified. Yet Jones might put into the literature "carnarvonite" after his Welsh home town, "helenite" after his girl friend, "polarisite" because the stuff is magnetic and glittery, or whatever else. Plenty of real minerals have lovely names; think of aventurine, sapphire, lapis lazuli, serpentine, onyx. If the writer can invent comparable ones, he will have added color to his story.

When there are plants and animals, boundless possibilities open up. But too many writers lazily ignore them. They mention grass, for instance, though the grasses form a distinct family which has not always been around on Earth and is no more likely to have developed on any other planet than are men, fiddler crabs, sequoias, or lactobacilli. In fact, while conceivably parallel evolution elsewhere has duplicated classes as broad as mammals or mosses, this too seems extremely improbable. Form follows function; therefore we can believe in many outward similarities, which might well cause humans to apply misnomers like "bird" or "bramble." But almost certainly, a biologist could point out variations that make the resemblances as superficial as those between shark and whale, or far more so. And in all events, exotic names help create an exotic atmosphere.

Some will be descriptive in their own right, with little else needed to evoke an image. If I may mention a few of my own, "crownbuck" is supposed to indicate a large and handsome horned animal, "flittery" a creature looking not unlike a moth, "braidbark" and "copperwood" two kinds of trees; names for flowerlike plants such as "kiss-me-never," for fruits such as "newton fig," and for beasts such as "sea preacher" may add a touch of poesy or humor. Referring again to classical dictionaries, I came up with plants like glycophyllon (sweetbranch) and animals like the macrotrach (longneck). A thickly armored, spike-tailed creature got the name "hoplite," from the heavy infantryman of ancient Greece, while one with fancy plumage came to be called "jackadandy." By exercising their imaginations, my colleagues can surely do better than this. Several already have.

The suffix "-oid," meaning "similar to," is useful but often abused. A thing like "rabbitoid" merely betrays lack of that same imagination, besides being an etymological horror. I suggest that, as a rule, the suffix should be reserved for rather general categories, and for Greek roots whenever possible. This would give us "theroid" to indicate animals that exhibit certain analogies to the terrestrial mammals, "herpetoid" (reptiles), "ornithoid" or "ptenoid" (birds), "ichthyoid" (fish), and so on. "Humanoid," though a bit unfortunate, seems too firmly entrenched to get rid of, especially since "anthropoid" and "android" are pre-empted.

In the rather unlikely event of people catching an extraterrestrial disease – or of a mutation of an existing germ afflicting them – a name like "the Blue Plague" seems unoriginal at this late date. How about "azuria" instead? And slang might make it "the blue staggers." In this case as elsewhere, a little disciplined whimsy should pay off for the writer, helping to convince the reader that here is more than a slightly edited copy of what he already knows.

Latin, Greek and English are not the only languages that ever existed or ever will. Judicious use of the rest can add richness. Thus, on a planet colonized largely by Germans, I put a creature they called the "dolchzahn" (daggertooth), while on another planet where the language descended from Serbo-Croatian, people gave the name of "zmayi" (dragons) to a race of beings who vaguely resembled tyrannosaurs. Again, a two-way dictionary is a versatile tool.

Intelligent natives will presumably have their own words for everything in sight; but that matter can be reserved for the general question of imaginary tongues.

Euphony and Geography

A world also has topographical features. Many on Earth bear haunting names; consider the Neversummer Mountains or the Smoke That Thunders (Victoria Falls). J. R. R. Tolkien constructed fine analogues, e.g., Mirkwood and Mount Weathertop. But the absolute master of nomenclature is Jack Vance. Only recall a handful of his out of many: Starbreak Fell, the High Jambles, the Apathetic Ocean; almost familiar Kirstendale, Barch Spike, Aerlith; wholly invented, singing names like Embelyon, Kaiin, Ampridatvir. In composing the last of these kinds, Lord Dunsany was equally brilliant — Merimna, Rhistaun, Bethmoora, Perdóndaris —

The sheer flow of such words lends magic. Occasionally a writer with a good ear employs, on purpose, a harsh sound, like E. R. Eddison's "Eshgrar Ogo" for an enemy stronghold, or one with parts that are suggestive, like Mervyn Peake's "Gormenghast" for his huge and eerie mansion, or one with a beat and clang, like Fletcher Pratt's "Skogalang" for the scene of a battle. But unless there is a similar reason to avoid it, musicality is advisable. Though not everybody has the innate talent for this which the authors do whom I have been citing, any writer worth his salt should be able to cultivate some sense of euphony.

Besides natural geography, an inhabited world will have places that people have built. In naming these, the same principles of freshness, plausibility and sound can greatly assist in weaving the spell. If we are to use English, a study of the North American map will show us how varied, picturesque, and historically informative the name of a town can be – as with Yellowknife, Port Radium, Deadwood, Santa Fé, Medicine Hat, Fort Defiance, New Orleans. Within various communities we find areas like Chinatown, the Citadel, Columbus Circle, buildings like the Alamo, the Space Needle, Ghirardelli Square, thoroughfares like Wall Street, Maiden Lane, Cannery Row. Needless to say, countries besides the USA and Canada have abundant examples of their own. However, in older lands, or where a new population has tried to continue an ancient name, generally the meanings are lost or nearly lost, and the effect resembles that of an invented language.

For a remote planet or future, is it too much trouble to work out something like, say, Damnation Alley opening onto Half Moon Street, which in turn proceeds to Velvet Circus in the wealthiest part of Silverville? These illustrations I have deliberately made up on the spot. With a little work, it is possible to do much better.

Again, a real but foreign language can add both glamour and depth, as in Karen Anderson's "Treaty in Tartessos," where the centaurs speak a version of Basque and thus make the small fantasy imply much more than it overtly says.

Adam's Art

Dwellers in our fictional regions should develop ways of getting along together — customs, institutions, organizations, public offices, all of which they will name. Jack Vance's game of hussade, pageant of The Viewing of Antique Tabards, and caste of sacerdotes are splendid cases in point. Likewise, when Malcolm Jameson gave to a fictional head of government the title "Autarch," it was immediately clear that that government was a one-man dictatorship, and had been for a considerable time.

People, human or nonhuman, will also possess individual and, usually, family names. If these are the same sort as today's, the same common sense rules apply as do in here-and-now fiction. First, to avoid embarrassing the subject and possibly getting sued, the writer should never knowingly employ the name of a living person. I go so far as to check this out in local telephone directories, or in that of a distant city if a character is said to reside there. The precaution does not guarantee against a crank legal action, but reduces the chance, and ought to help the defense should worst come to worst.

Second, unfairly but truly, names have connotations. A man called, say, Archibald Phipps may well be as brave as a lion, but to maintain this of a fictional person is to invite guffaws (unless, perhaps, his heroism is shown as compensation for the handicap his parents wished on him). Now today it would be considered crude to christen thus a simpering fool, or to dub a brawny adventurer Thorstein Hardman. Nevertheless, there is a reasonable range within which the name can to some degree suggest the personality and so reinforce the image, as with P. G. Wodehouse's Bertram Wooster or, at the opposite end and in science fiction, Gordon R. Dickson's Donal Graeme.

In any case, including that majority of names that are more or less neutral, they should not form a jarring combination, e.g., "Chloris Simpson," which puts "-is" straight up against "Si-." And unless it is absolutely necessary, no two characters in a given story should have names which look at all alike. Indeed, if possible, to minimize the chance of reader confusion, none should begin with the same letter.

Nor should names be overly familiar. An occasional Smith or Thompson is okay, maybe even essential for verisimilitude. But with slight effort, a writer can find many that are less common in America and therefore more interesting and memorable to the American reader — Ashcroft, Blenkiron,

Lanthier, to pick three of British origin at random. And, of course, out yonder is a planetful of people called Avelan, Benavente, Kalehua, M'Kato, Nishanian, Shi, Uraiqat, Xepoleas. . . . The directory of a large city, the footnotes in a major scientific journal, or encyclopedia articles on the history and literature of various countries are good sources of names, provided one changes the given names. I think that science fiction should be especially conscious of the fact that the future will not belong exclusively to Anglo-Saxons.

Nor will it preserve names in their present forms forever. Some do last an astonishingly long time with little or no change, like "Einar" in Scandinavia or "Huang" in China. And sometimes archaic ones are resurrected, particularly in countries like Ireland and Israel. But oftenest they metamorphose, like "Caesar" becoming "Cesare" in Italy (or, as a title, "Kaiser" in Germany, "Tsar" in Russia). This evolution can go in numerous directions. The most obvious case is the Hebrew "Yohanaan," which we know as "John" or "Jack" but which is also "Ioannes," "Johann," "Hans," "Jan," "Jens," "Jean," "Juan," "Giovanni," "Ivan," "Evan" and on and on, including the female versions. Eventually a name will vanish altogether; hardly anybody today is called "Amenhotep," "Sennacherib," or "Nezahualcoyotl."

Projecting into the future, science fiction writers who postulate multiethnic combinations like "Samuel I. Hayakawa" or, for that matter, "Poul Anderson," are not describing anything new. Something offbeat like, say, "Boris Ramanujan" might indicate a contact between certain peoples that has not yet taken place on any large scale — though this gimmick has perhaps been overworked. More interesting may be the transformations of the names themselves; but guesses about that must be made with care if the results are to be convincing. For instance, because of where the accent falls, "Howard" is most unlikely to become "Whard," but might possibly become "Hower" and, at last, "How." If "Smith" turns into

"Smeeth" or "Smit," this will probably be part of an overall shift in the language which simultaneously changes "Timothy" into "Teemothy" or "Timoty." There are always exceptions, so we cannot safely be dogmatic; yet a reasonably consistent pattern of mutations is more believable than a few arbitrary mutilations.

In the quite far future (or past) of man, among the natives of remote planets, and in the realms of Faerie, we may expect to find names that are completely unrelated to those we know. When these belong to individuals, the same basic principles apply as for places. We can "translate" back into English and get such romantic coinages as William Rotsler's "Windbird" and "Starbringer." Or we can cut loose altogether, with Dunsany and Vance for our masters, to get excellencies like Mohontis, Lirazel, Ethodea, Pallis Atwrode — though again an unusual ear is required if this is to be done really well. Too many authors merely produce monosyllabic grunts, polysyllabic gabble, or things that are inoffensive but dull for lack of any music. By giving their business closer attention, they could much improve the product.

Intermediately, we can create names, and associated words, in an imaginary language by basing this on a real one. L. Sprague de Camp pioneered the method with great success in his Viagens Interplanetarias stories. There the principal tongue of the planet Krishna is derived from Persian, leading to place names like Gozashstand and personal names like Zei. More recently, Frank Herbert did the same thing with Arabic in his famous *Dune*.

For this we need not be linguists. A detailed map of a given language area will provide enough information for our purposes, a general feel for the material and a supply of syllables which we can then modify and reshuffle. An advantage of the procedure is that these invented words will show a certain interrelationship — a unique character — that is otherwise difficult if not impossible to obtain, and that makes our creation readily distinguishable. For example, in *Fire Time* I based the speech of two different societies on Ethiopian and Inuit respectively, to get contrasting sets like "Larreka, Wolua, Beronnen" versus "Arnanak, Evisakuk, Narvu." Whether I succeeded or not is for readers to judge. Certainly the method requires care and diligence.

But so does every other means and aspect of nomenclature; and it is only a small part, although important, of the whole job of creation, or even Creation. When Adam named the animals, he had barely started his checkered career. Nevertheless, this *was* very nearly the first thing he did.

This is the first of two articles in this volume that deal with the possible futures of Earth. New writers have often fallen into the trap of simply tacking onto the present a few fancy gadgets, a rocketship or two, and a Bug-Eyed Monster and calling it science fiction. Unfortunately, as a study of even recent history will show, this has not been nor will it be the case for a number of future Earths. **Dr. Jerry Pournelle** *tackles this common error among new writers from the technological and broader sociological standpoint, and has come up with material that every writer must be aware of if he hopes to convince the editors of Analog, Galaxy and all the rest that his story is indeed worth publishing.*

Dr. Pournelle, Ph.D., is a former space scientist and Director of Special Studies (AEROSPACE Corporation), former SFWA President, winner of the 1971 John W. Campbell Award, Galaxy Magazine Science Editor and five-time nominee for the Hugo Award. In addition to all this, he is coauthor with Larry Niven of one of the biggest and most popular SF books of the decade — The Mote in God's Eye — has four children and a beautiful wife, Roberta, and is currently working on five more collaborations with Mr. Niven.

CHAPTER 6:

Building Future Worlds: Logic and Consistency in the Craft of Science Fiction

by
Jerry Pournelle

There are a lot of different kinds of science fiction. If we accept the term *speculative* fiction preferred by some writers, there are even more. Under the banner of science fiction, we can find: pure fantasy; sword and sorcery, with or without barbarian heroes and complaisant heroines; grey stories about grey people sitting in grey chambers 7.63 meters below ground, thinking grey thoughts and listening to grey music; super-science epics and space opera; detective stories set in the future or on other worlds; straight adventure stories, ditto; idea stories; attempts to predict the future; anti-utopian stories warning us away from some trend the author finds ominous; satires; stories that not even the author seems to understand;

stories that turn out to be madmen's dreams; I could go on for another page or so.

Not all of these create future worlds, and of those that do try to present a future world, not all have anything to do with logic and consistency. Even so, logic and consistency are important to science fiction; many of the best SF stories ever done have been meticulously worked out and are utterly realistic. Even purely speculative stories must generally have *some* limits to speculation, some internal consistency, some correspondence with today's realities. A story in which anything goes is generally dull. What possible conflict can develop if anything is possible? We want to surprise and amaze the reader, but not by simply throwing in new ideas at random. Even fantasy has a logic, and some of the best fantasy employs much the same techniques as are needed to write about "realistic" futures.

Science fiction is not prediction. True, SF writers have done about as well at predicting the future as have economists, historians and politicians; but that's only to say that most "predictions" of the future are just plain wrong. If you have a working crystal ball, you can use it to get rich. You don't need to write science fiction.

Even so, a good part of science fiction is intended to be realistic. It is this kind of SF that this chapter is concerned with. Some of my remarks may be applicable to fantasies, satires, and other varieties of SF that are not supposed to be "believable"; but for the most part, I am talking about "classical" SF, the "Old Wave" straight stuff; stories that neither reader nor author thinks *will* happen, but both believe *can* or even *might* happen. This kind of story must be at least consistent, and generally should also be logical.

By logical I mean we can get there from here: the story is set in a world that is possible. Given what we know now, and trends that we see now, the alternate future of the story *could* happen, even if it probably won't.

By consistent I mean internal consistency: the story's parts hang together. The society or social order in the story is compatible with the way the characters act; the technology and science in the story is consistent with itself; and perhaps most important of all, the social order and the technology are consistent with each other.

Before anyone screams foul, I want to repeat that there are other kinds of SF. Some "speculative" fiction writers, for example, argue that logic and consistency are straight jackets; SF, they say, ought to be "free," and writers need not worry about how many false assumptions they make. SF is a literature in which all mechanical restraints should be forgotten.

Now sometimes this produces a good story. Harlan Ellison, for example, is noted for stories that have no internal logic at all. His "Boy and His Dog" is shot through with inconsistencies, and the ending depends on the reader's believing something that 30 seconds of reflection would show is physiologically ridiculous. Ellison is far more concerned with emotional impact than good sense, yet he is one of the most popular SF writers alive.

This proves nothing. Ellison has a command of the language that is beyond most writers. The allegorical stories he produces are hardly typical. If you can write like Ellison, you need no advice on how to write. However, most of us aren't Ellisons, and a lot of those who think they are wonder why they're slowly starving to death. In many ways "speculative" fiction requires a great deal more creative genius than does the most logically developed traditional story.

A moderately successful "Old Wave" traditional story which develops ideas logically and consistently can be salable and even enjoyable without being brilliant; an only moderately good New Wave "speculative fiction" piece is often a godawful mess. But though the traditional form can be written without genius, it cannot be written without *work*. If "realistic" SF does not always demand brilliance, it does demand meticulous attention to detail, reasonable familiarity with both science and human behavior, and a good bit of skull sweat. Probably the worst science fiction of all results from attempts at realism by writers just too lazy to do their homework.

Technological Consistency

The first task is keeping the science self-consistent. This is often the most difficult task for new writers with little or no scientific background. Failure to keep the story's science consistent also produces the most hilarious boners, and the most letters, of all. Fans and readers will almost always spot this kind of error, and they are never shy about telling the writer, often in published letters.

There is no magic formula for avoiding these errors. Of course it helps to know some science, but even this isn't infallible: Larry Niven, who knows his stuff, managed to get the Earth rotating in the wrong direction in the first editions of *Ringworld*. In Niven's case it was sheer carelessness; obviously he knows better. I could give examples from writers who don't know any better.

If a writer knows no science, he'd better admit it and get some advice from someone who does. There is no excuse for some of the stupidities that get into SF stories.

Sure: science fiction is fiction about science. We are permitted inventions now thought impossible, and technical achievements not now expected. But we are not permitted just any old invention or achievement; there is a logic to these things. The most far-out science is still science, not fantasy. Except for the specifics assumed for the story, the rest of the universe should be left alone. Certain inventions force certain developments, and that logic must be maintained; but we must not assume that in science fiction all bets are off and everything is permitted.

For example: the conservation laws, and the resulting laws

of thermodynamics, are basic to modern science. Unless violation of those laws is specifically assumed for the story — and the writer points this out — the reader has a right to assume that these important principles still hold. It's no fair resolving a plot by having the characters invent a gadget that works by perpetual motion — unless the writer shows that he has thereby tossed out nearly everything physicists think they know.

This rules out a number of "inventions." Examples: plant men, in all their guises. One form of plant men is the magic enzyme that allows human beings to breathe carbon dioxide instead of oxygen. After all, plants on Earth do it; why shouldn't men be able to? So the author reasons, and out comes a story in which men happily rush about on Mars breathing in CO_2 and eating normal food, climbing mountains, and indeed acting as men generally do. Why not?

Energy is why not. Plants take in CO_2 and give off oxygen, but they do it by presenting a very large surface area to the Sun. They absorb sunlight and use that energy to break CO_2 into carbon and oxygen. Later they use oxygen to burn carbon for heat energy. Plants spend most of their lives doing this. They are low-energy organisms, and their leaves are not superfluous; their lack of mobility is dictated because they just can't take in enough sunlight. If intelligent mobile plants could exist in this part of the solar system, they'd exist on Earth. No magic treatment will enable men to breathe in carbon dioxide and rush about Mars as if they were breathing oxygen. Actually, given the low pressures on Mars, even Martian plants have a big problem: in order to suck in enough CO_2 they'll have to be the organic equivalents of vacuum cleaners, and have enormous leaf surfaces to catch the lower energy sunlight that hits the fourth planet. Plant men on Mars would have to grow leaves or plug their big toes into the light socket, or perform some other marvelous trick to get enough energy to move around.

Another example: the "Dean Drive." This was, many will recall, a device that supposedly took rotary acceleration, as in an electric drill motor, and turned it into linear acceleration, as in a rocket ship. It was an exciting idea: with such an "antigravity" device you could hook up a Drive to a nuclear sub and fly the thing directly to the Moon.

Marvelous. Incidentally, although there are still fans who believe that the big industries somehow suppressed the Dean Drive, the truth is that several aerospace outfits wanted to buy it — but were never given a demonstration that convinced them the thing worked. Hardly surprising, because the discovery of a gizmo like that would mean that a lot of what we think we know about physics just isn't so.

There's no reason to think we know everything, of course; surely there's more to be discovered than we've already found out. But if a story does postulate a reactionless drive, it should also postulate some pretty strange physical effects. We have here a gadget that somehow exerts a force in a way entirely different from anything we've ever imagined. Consistency demands that the writer use it for more than just space ships.

The Dean Drive, if it worked, would have demanded a partial restructuring of physics, but it wasn't a full antigravity machine. Antigravity wouldn't partially restructure physics: it would make hash out of Relativity. General Relativity states that gravity isn't a "force" at all; it's a phenomenon due to the geometry of space. Thus it cannot possibly be countered unless our whole notion of space-time is wrong. Once again, consistency demands that if a writer introduces a device that is impossible by current physical theory, he must give some thought to the side effects. When Einstein invented Relativity he was concerned with photoelectric effects and slight changes in the orbit of the planet Mercury. The result was $e = mc^2$, which had something more than a theoretical impact on our lives. A working antigravity device would demand a comparable restructuring of physical knowledge, and that would have effects at least as far-reaching as those of nuclear weapons.

There are less complex examples of technological consistency. Some will be discussed in other chapters of this book. Obviously, for example, you can't have a planet with both free hydrogen and free oxygen in its atmosphere, because hydrogen burns in oxygen. Yet a bunch of anthropologists who ought to know better did just that in a book called *Cultures Beyond the Earth.*

Technological consistency is at bottom a matter of having a feel for the sciences; of knowing enough about various disciplines such as physics, chemistry and biology to be able to distinguish between inventions that *develop* present theories and those that overthrow them; and having made the distinction, dealing appropriately with each type. The rocket ship, for example, embodies no physics not known in Newton's time; an engineer with the right tools and materials could have built the Apollo capsule a hundred years ago. Atomic energy, on the other hand, required basic new theories; atom bombs aren't even possible in nineteenth century physics.

How does one get a feel for the sciences, then? I fear there is nothing for it but some hard work. It isn't necessary to take a formal degree in science; a number of "Old Wave" writers, like Gordon Dickson, have little classroom education outside the humanities (and some, unlike Dickson, have no formal education at all.) It *is* necessary to read widely. Various "popular" books on the sciences will help. Regular attention to *Scientific American* is vital if only because one must assume that one's readers are familiar with it. Membership in the Library of Science Book Club is useful.

At the end of this chapter I'll include a short bibliography of books that can help. They won't do the whole job nor are all required reading, but at least they can show new writers some of the pitfalls.

Social Structures

In the early days of SF, authors could ignore "future history." They could merely assume that things would go on much as they always have. Heinlein, for example, wrote future histories in the forties — and his stories made few changes in the way people lived. "The Man Who Sold The Moon" lives in a business community where judges hold court, county fairs are still popular entertainment, marriage and the family are the normal institutions of man-woman relationships; women blush at strong language, and puritanism is an important factor in public relations. This is not to criticize Heinlein: I use him as an example precisely because he was perhaps the best writer of that period.

It is difficult to write that kind of story today. The world seems a much less stable place than it did in the forties and fifties, or for that matter, even the sixties. Women's rights, civil rights, participatory democracy, antiwar sentiments, total decline of patriotism, progressive breakup of family structure, ordinariness of crime (when I was a boy there had been only one unsolved murder in my city in ten years), radical changes in conventional morality — all of these and dozens of more trends will have an effect on the social order of the future, and a writer must think about each one before constructing a background for his story.

No matter how isolated his characters may be from the rest of the human race, the sociology of the future is going to affect the story. If there is a scientific expedition to a far place, is it mostly male, mostly female, or coed? If coed, how does this affect the relationships of crew members? Are they polite to members of the opposite sex? One assumes that sexual urges will not die away; what kind of shipboard morality prevails? Is casual and recreational sex the norm? If so, how does that change the depth of feeling between man and woman? What has happened to marriage and the family? If the family has withered away, who raised the story's characters, and how has this strange (to us) childhood affected them? If "broken home" can be cited by social workers as an excuse for gangsterism in the present era, what are people like in a time when there are no homes to be broken? These are questions that cannot be ignored. In the past it was all right to have Lance Stirling, Science Officer of an all-male crew, raised in a middle-class family and imbued with middle-class morals and ethics; but today any writer presenting Commander Stirling as real had better be prepared to defend his assumptions about the kind of world that produced him.

The motivations of the characters depend on their backgrounds, and the backgrounds cannot seem impossible to the reader. This means that an SF writer has to do some hard thinking. Just how much of human motivation stems from our social order? From half-remembered commands such as "Thou Shalt Not Steal," and "Honor Thy Father and Thy Mother"? From the universal brotherhood that is at least implied by Christianity, so that we at least feel guilty about thinking of another human being as "fair game," an object, a thing, a victim?

There is a lot of inconsistent nonsense presented as science fiction, and many of the inconsistencies come from failure to think about the problem of human motivation. If the society described (or assumed) in the story is brutal and ugly and rejects bourgeois morality, how can the characters continue to act as if they'd grown up in Searcy, Arkansas?

Turn of the Wheel

Building a consistent future is hard work; so hard that many SF writers, including myself, sketch out the social order before we even attempt the story. Is courage a virtue in this future world? Are there virtues at all? Why? What do men and women strive for, and do the sexes have the same goals? And it is no good throwing together a batch of social assumptions at random, either. Although each may be logical in that some trend in that direction can be seen in today's world, the total effect may be utterly inconsistent. A social order must hang together; if it is too ugly, or provides no motivation for people to keep it together, it will fall apart and something else will take its place. There have been revolutionaries in every society; most revolutions fail; but unless there are at least *some* defenders of the social order, it is doomed. A society can endure the indifference of many of its members, but not of all of them; it can endure a number of contradictions, but give it too many and it won't last long enough to write a story about it.

It is here that we approach controversy. In my judgment, there are few new trends in modern political thought. If we look into history, we can find many eras in which religion was not taken very seriously; when the family was thought old-fashioned and outmoded; when continuous progress was assumed to be inevitable, so that we would never again return to the bad old days of aristocracy and monarchy; when democracy was the inevitable wave of the future; when all men and women would have rights, and slavery was ended forever. Yet in each case the wheel has turned again. Women's rights have come and gone. The Roman Republic became Empire. The Golden Age of Athens lasted about two generations.

In 1975 fewer people lived under democracy than in 1932. Even as I write this, both personal dictatorship and hereditary government are emerging in India; most of Africa and South America are ruled by armies, Spain has restored the Monarchy with the fervent blessing of at least a large minority if not a majority; the Shah of Iran seems firmly established as one of the most powerful men on Earth; and few Americans would give long odds that John-John Kennedy will not some day be President of the US, although at the moment not one of us has the foggiest notion of what kind of ruler he would make.

Yet each time the wheel has turned, it has not gone back to its old position. The Roman Empire was not the Monarchy, nor yet one of the Eastern despotisms. The Holy Roman Empire was not the Roman Empire. The military dictatorships of Africa and South America are not duplicates of those garrison states Plato described as Timocracy. We can postulate futures in which past forms of order have been restored, but they will be subtly or wildly different.

Think It Through

When you write about social orders of the future, you are bound to be controversial because you are writing about politics. A militant democrat will reject stories about future Empires because he believes Democracy is on the march and inevitably must triumph; writers who say something else can work just as well are challenging his beliefs. Oddly enough it is less controversial to postulate future dictatorships, fascist states, and truly ugly societies than it is to postulate some kind of tranquil aristocratic state. I suspect this is because in the ugly societies the characters generally burn with revolutionary fervor — and if they don't, they ought to! — whereas in stories of future Empire, the populace is generally reasonably happy. Those who believe in inevitable "progress" can be persuaded that something has sidetracked the millennium — but not that there never was and never will be a perfect social order.

Feminists become enraged when SF stories assume that there has been a turn of the wheel and renewed emphasis on different roles for the different sexes. Atheists do a slow burn if a story shows religious people in a future era. And so forth.

Since there is no universal agreement on what futures are logical, we can only attempt to make them consistent, and not too wildly improbable, although the most improbable societies can work for a story if the writer is good enough.

Take, for example, Heinlein's " 'If This Goes On . . .'." published in *Astounding* in 1940; this story assumes that the US has fallen under the dictatorship of a fundamentalist sect. No one today believes that is probable, likely or even possible; but it is presented in such detail, with the parts fitted together so well, that it is believable. And it does not contradict itself: however corrupted it has become, the ideal of the ruling elite, and thus the ideal taught in schools to the populace, is Christian, and the revolutionaries of the story need no fundamental restructuring of their childhood beliefs in order to oppose the government.

It is this kind of consistency that made Heinlein a master of science fiction. It is unfortunately rare. Although there are no universal agreements on what makes for a consistent social order, far too many writers seem not to have thought about the problem at all. For example: there are dozens of stories about an overcrowded Earth, in which the Population Control Bureau or some such agency rigidly dictates who can have how many children; illegal childbearing is a terrible crime; the populace itself hates parenthood and a man confessing to having two children will be beaten to death by drunks in a bar — and yet this is supposed to have gone on for a considerable period of time. Obviously that can't happen; if there is rigid population control, within the life span of one human the population will have declined. The situation simply isn't stable.

Another common example: the "devil theory" story, in which the agents of the anti-utopia are stupid, cowardly and incompetent, yet the state remains all-powerful while the populace seethes with hatred. Now not all social orders are internally consistent, and there have been remarkably stable governments filled with people who don't seem very bright; but there must be a reason for this. Perhaps most people don't care. They stay drunk and watch free entertainment; either Roman circuses or TV. Yet even in that kind of tranquilized and emotion-drained state, there must be *some* efficiencies. The liquor must be distilled, the tranquilizers distributed, the entertainments organized. No government is more than a couple of meals away from rioting and revolution; *somebody* has got to grow crops and distribute food. Those who do the work must have *some* motivation. So must the soldiers and police who maintain the social order.

If This Goes On . . . .

There are no set rules for building a logical and consistent future society. Indeed, the ability to do that job is one of the prerequisites for becoming a science fiction writer, and if you don't understand what I'm talking about here, perhaps some other line of work would be more congenial.

Yet societies condition and change human motivations, and unless one has some feel for human motivation, it is unlikely that he can be a writer at all, whether SF or mainstream. Thus the SF writer needs some feel for history and sociology, or else he had best stick to societies he knows and not dream up new ones. This has been the failure of some of the most scientific of SF writers; even the hardest technical "idea" story requires some attention to social details, and without that the story is unbelievable. On the other hand, some of the finest science fiction has been purely sociological.

A Canticle for Leibowitz, for example, assumes no scientific marvels; indeed, except for World War III, there is no technological development at all. Instead we have a struggle to keep what little knowledge remains after the war. Even better examples are *1984* and *Brave New World;* although each of these famous novels employed a few technological devices not widespread when the books were written, technology is nearly irrelevant in them. The point of the books is to examine what might happen if certain social trends continue.

Brave New World and *1984* are examples of a class of SF known as "If this goes on" stories. This kind of story assumes that one or more present-day trends will continue to a logical end. The effectiveness of the story depends on the writer's ability to make the resulting social order both logical and consistent; to make it seem real to the reader. Although there are plenty of satires the authors never intend anyone to take seriously, Orwell and Huxley are frightening precisely because they can make us believe that their worlds really could come about. We can imagine a world without spiritual values and whose order is built in Freudian psychology; we can imagine a boot stamping on a human face forever.

The Wealth of the Template

Once again, there is no magic formula for the writer; the best advice I can offer is to work hard. The writer should be aware of a great deal more about his imaginary society than ever gets into the story. When Larry Niven and I wrote *Mote in God's Eye* we ended up with almost as many pages of unpublished (and unpublishable) notes as were in the book. That work shows (or we like to think it does), but only indirectly. Our detailed human and alien social structures allowed us, whenever our characters were faced with decisions, to have the characters act consistently. It was a lot of work to create those worlds, but having done it, the work of writing the novel was immeasurably easier. Of course *Mote* was a big novel, and thus justified the detail work put into its planning; short stories and novelets can't be done in so much detail because the writer would starve to death. It is for this reason that many writers, including Niven, Anderson, Haldeman, Heinlein and myself, write a number of short stories in "templates" — that is, we write different stories, using different characters, but all set into one carefully created future. The template takes a lot of work to create; but once that work has been done, the writer has an inexhaustible mine to draw upon for years to come.

The Interaction of Technology and Society

Describing the effects of technology on humanity is one of the primary goals of science fiction; a large part of the SF readership finds this the most important and most interesting facet of SF. Unfortunately it is all too often done superficially.

As an example, take energy sources; many stories of the future postulate hydrogen fusion plants. Now hydrogen is plentiful, and the plants will put out a lot of electricity; energy in a fusion society will be relatively cheap. There can be no energy crisis unless one is artificially created; what motivates the creators of the crisis?

A society with cheap energy is likely to be affluent. There will be plenty of building materials. Fertilizers, which are easily produced given cheap energy, will allow abundant harvests; since there is cheap energy for pumping and water reclamation, agriculture will be less dependent on weather than it is now. Under those circumstances, is it likely that people will be sleeping in abandoned movie houses?

If you want to postulate plentiful and cheap energy and an economy of scarcity, you've got some thinking to do. How can this be? Is the economy controlled and the situation deliberate? Why? From what motive? Are people breeding so fast that they absorb all resources as fast as they're created? Whatever approach is chosen, it will say a lot about the government of that period. Why doesn't the government control population? Not strong enough? Then this can hardly be a story of an evil fascist dictatorship. And so forth.

Another example, worked out in great detail by Larry Niven: suppose a reliable means of teleportation has been discovered. To get from one place to another, it is only necessary to insert a credit card into the phone, and dial the address where you want to go. You vanish to reappear where you've dialed. This invention is obviously going to do strange things to civilization. What will happen to all the automobiles? To that enormous concrete grid — vaster than the Pyramids — which we call the Interstate Highway system? To all those people now employed in auto manufacturing, maintenance, fueling, fuel refining, fuel discovering, sales?

A story in which everyone teleports is feasible. A story in that world that opens with the hero riding in a passenger car has got a problem.

Another SF gimmick: small and cheap fusion-powered spaceships. Typically these serve asteroid frontiersmen — "Belters" — the way horses served cowboys. The Belter gets a ship and goes prospecting for rare metals.

OK, so far; but observe. The ship is not a horse. It wasn't produced by breeding two other ships. It's a very complex machine that generates more power than Con Ed. It contains a gizmo capable of containing a thermonuclear reaction. How can it possibly be cheap enough for the average roughneck prospector to own?

The ship's drive contains a magic field that can hold onto the thermonuclear reaction on one side, and let the force of the reaction escape from the other; there's got to be a rocket effect or all the power in the world won't move the ship (unless the prospector has a Dean Drive in good working order). Moreover, each of those prospectors has a thermonuclear weapon at his disposal; he can hold any city on Earth at hazard, and if it doesn't pay, Zap! Thus there *must* be a mechanism of social control.

Technology changes society. It may not change it in obvious ways: one of the most significant effects of the automobile was on marriage, dating, and sexual mores. SF writers are no more likely to be successful at predicting the effects of technology than were social scientists able to predict what Henry Ford's innovations would do to the divorce rate, but they must at least try. After all, we are writing fiction, not forecasting the future. If we are logical and consistent, if we make our future world plausible to the reader, we have done our job.

We are not doing our job if we merely dash off any old thing that comes into our heads. Building logical and consistent worlds takes work, and lots of it; but take heart, the work is never wasted. Thinking about ways to keep the asteroid prospector from holding Rio de Janeiro to ransom will probably influence the story and make the plot easier; thinking about the ways the characters interact with that government will give new insights into the characters; and so forth.

In fact, playing the logic and consistency game can be so much fun that the writer gets fascinated to the detriment of output. I used to spend hours drawing maps in meticulous detail when all I needed was a crude sketch. Even that wasn't wasted, though, and some minor details that seemed to fit into my map ended up as a vital part of the story. Every SF writer has had this happen to him.

Moreover, thinking about your future world is a different kind of work from sitting at the typewriter and pounding out the story itself. Approached with the right attitude, it can be a lot of fun; and it's a very good game to play when you're suffering from what Randall Garrett calls "writer's snowblindness" — the blindness that results from vast acres of blank white paper. Most of us at one time or another suffer from "writer's block," and of course the ability to get around that occupational hazard is what distinguishes professional writers from those who merely play at writing. As a remedy for writer's block, I can strongly recommend creating a future world. A world created in enough logical and consistent detail is vastly exciting and practically cries for a story; and if *that* won't get the fingers moving across the typewriter keys, well, maybe selling shoes isn't such a bad way to make a living after all . . . .

Recommended Works:

Asimov, Isaac. *Asimov's Guide to Science.* New York: Basic
    Books, 1972.

Bretnor, Reginald. *Science Fiction Today and Tomorrow.* New
    York: Harper & Row, 1974.

Bruce-Briggs, B., and Kahn, Herman. *Things to Come.* New
    York: Macmillan, 1972.

de Camp, L. Sprague. *The Ancient Engineers.* New York:
    Ballantine, 1974.

Dole, S. H. *Habitable Planets for Man.* New York: American
    Elsevier, 1970.

Hartmann, William. *Moons and Planets.* Belmont, California:
    Wadsworth, 1972.

Sagan, Carl. *The Cosmic Connection.* New York: Doubleday,
    1973.

*This is the companion piece to "Building Future Worlds."
In this article,* **Gardner Dozois** *explores in detail the CHAR-
ACTER development side of creating a logical and consistent
future. It is extremely safe to say here that there isn't an editor
in the field who will buy a story that is thinly disguised Roman
History dressed up to look as though it is taking place a thousand
years in the future. Yet these same editors receive thousands
of such manuscripts every year from writers who do not know
any better. "Living the Future" is designed, then, to assist you
in avoiding this pitfall — again, emphasizing the people who
will inhabit your future world.*

*Gardner Dozois, a Philadelphian of some repute, is undoubt-
edly one of the most popular newer writers in science fiction.
His novelets and shorter works have been consistently nominated
for the highest awards in the field; he has been a reader for
Galaxy Magazine, has served in Germany in the Army, and
has just had his first novel (in collaboration with George Alec
Effinger) published by Berkley Books — Nightmare Blue.*

CHAPTER 7:

Living the Future: You Are What You Eat

by
Gardner Dozois

For a number of years I worked for the *Galaxy* group of magazines as a "slush pile" reader, evaluating the endless flow of unsolicited manuscripts — sometimes as many as a hundred a day — that come into a magazine or publishing house and end up heaped in filing cabinets or cardboard boxes: the slush pile. I read thousands of manuscripts — from duds to instant classics to near misses to outright plagiarisms — and I'm here to tell you that, with the exception of those turned down because they were illiterate or indecipherable, most of the science fiction stories that came into the slush pile were rejected because they suffered from what I came to call the 1950 Syndrome.

You can easily recognize such material. It's A.D. 2653, and yet people drive around in gasoline-fueled automobiles with internal combustion engines, live in suburbia, shop in super-markets, subscribe to the Book-of-the-Month Club, and mow the lawn every weekend. For amusement they go to the movies, dances, barbecue, or sit at home and watch television. Every man has a crewcut; he is a soldier called "Captain,"

"Major" or "Sarge," or a teacher called "Professor." Or he is a wealthy, self-employed scientist who whips together world-saving devices out of scrap metal and bailing wire in his basement workshop, in which case he is called "Doc." More rarely is he a politician, and referred to by his title — "Worldmaster Jones," "Coordinator Grey"; or a bigwig white-collar businessman called "Mister Andrews," or whatever, by everyone, including his children and wife. No other professions exist. No women work except for an occasional snappy, wise-cracking, gum-chewing girl reporter, and this only until she marries the hero at the end of the story. The only other women who exist are dumb younger sisters of the hero, or the shy and sheltered daughters of atomic physicists with basement workshops. There are no races: everyone is white, middle-class, American, middle-of-the-road. No one has ever heard of homosexuality or drug addiction or pollution. People either use 20-year-old hipster slang ("cool," "you cats," "dig it") or they all say "gosh" and "darn" a lot. Everyone is unflaggingly and unquestionably patriotic. Everyone is smugly contented. They are all the most trusting of optimists.

You recognize this world, don't you? In spite of the calendar that reads A.D. 2653, it's certainly not the future. No. It's 1950. Or rather, an oversimplified and prettied-up version of 1950, distilled by the popular imagination from years of *Ozzie and Harriet, Father Knows Best,* and *Leave It To Beaver.* In an age that's seen Watergate, Watts, My Lai, the energy crisis, *Deep Throat,* sex-change operations, moon flights and women's liberation, it's hardly credible as the Past, let alone the Future.

And yet, stories reeking of the Syndrome turn up over and over again in the slush pile.

Why?

Well, after all, science fiction is pretty easy to write, isn't it? It's just a matter of using fancy names — just change the names, apply a thin layer of technologese and jargon, right? Say "helicar" instead of car, "helipad" instead of driveway, "tri-vid" instead of television, "feelies" (or "smellies," or "grabbies") instead of movies. Better still, use the word "space" as a prefix for everything: spacesuit, spacegun, space-helmet, spacehouse, spacedog, spacecow.... Right? Just change the names and you can write a confession-magazine love story, a cowboy story, a gothic, or a nurse novel, and sell it as science fiction. Right?

Wrong.

There's no better way to ensure that your story will not sell. Stories deeply tainted by the 1950 Syndrome are not science fiction; they do not do what science fiction should do — they are swindles. They are thin and transparent frauds that are almost automatically rejected by nearly every SF editor in the business. Even the most routine hack space opera demands and delivers more. They are the duds, the unsalable lowest denominator of the slush pile.

Future Schlock

Why do people of intelligence and talent turn out Syndrome stories when they first try their hand at writing science fiction?

Because of tunnel-vision. Because they know no better. Because they have not learned to unleash, discipline and control their imaginations. Because they simply have not been taught to look at a future society as a *real, self-consistent and organic thing.*

It works like this: a layman decides to write SF, and immediately starts to grope for a science-fictional idea. He reaches down into his subconscious, the well of creativity, and the first thing he hits is the vast harvest of concepts and assumptions and ideas he's gleaned over the years from all the bad comic books and horror movies and television shows that have been labeled Science Fiction. A moment's rational reflection should tell him that if the idea/image were floating about in the easily accessible part of the mind, it has probably been used to death in print years before — why else would it be such common property as to show up in the mind of someone with only the most casual of contacts with the genre? But he does not so reflect, because he's being mentally lazy, and so off the story goes. Like General MacArthur, it will return.

Thus, the layman, the one unfamiliar with the genre. But even the more habitual science fiction reader may fare no better. In fact, he is often more susceptible to the Syndrome, and may well be worse off than the layman — in addition to comics and the visual media, he must also cope with the sediment laid down by years of reading bad pulp space opera. This is why, 20 years or more after they've ceased to be commercially viable, the same old stock SF gimmicks, cousin-germane to the 1950 Syndrome stories, continue to march needlessly across editorial desks: vast Galactic Empires and the intrepid secret agents who single-handedly overthrow them; Bug-Eyed Monsters who lust after beautiful ladies; interstellar armadas banging away at each other so unimaginatively that you can almost hear the sails flapping. Stories wherein, in Harry Harrison's words, "Bright young things voyage out from Earth in miraculous ships that get anywhere in a flash, to alien planets with oxygen atmospheres where exotically-shaped aliens talk colloquial English and think exactly like their American counterparts. . . ." Kurt Vonnegut's Eliot Rosewater complains that science fiction writers "write about Earthlings all the time, and they're all Americans. Practically nobody on Earth is an American." Damon Knight asks, "Where is the space hero who is an Indian from India, or a black African, or a Maylay or a Chinese, or — all right, let's not ask too much — where is the hero who is Italian?"

Why aren't there different kinds of people and different ways of thought out among the stars? Why is the future 1950? Why doesn't anything *new* happen in these stories? Because bad fiction perpetuates itself, and stifles the imagination that might otherwise revitalize or replace it.

To write good SF today, you must go beyond all that. You must push further and harder, reach down deeper into your own mind until you break through into the strange and terrible country wherein live your own dreams, your own ideas and images, your own nightmares. You must reject easy answers, soggy and chewed-out questions, facile images that come too automatically to the fingertips. You must reject all the clichés that falsely masquerade as genre, skirt by the dead and burnt-out shells of what were once viable fictional structures.

You must come upon the future as if you'd just discovered it; you must look at it with new eyes. You must make it a real place, then visit and explore it.

The Cosmic Connection

The first step is a philosophical — almost a mystical — one; an act of faith, an exercise of will. You must retool your mind. You must teach your eyes to see. One of the premier values of science fiction as literature is that it enables us to look at ourselves through alien eyes. It enables us, as do few other forms of art, to see not only what is, but, submerged in it, what has been, and what will be: to perceive the linkages, the connections, the web of cause-and-effect that holds the world together. The *interdependence* of things. Today this is sometimes called "thinking ecologically," but SF writers knew about it long before ecology became fashionable, knew that in the long run (and sometimes the short) everything affects everything else, that Heisenberg's Principle can also be applied to people and to society.

This mental retooling is vital — I cannot emphasize its importance too much, especially for someone not well-read in the genre. It is the first step, and the biggest one; without it there is no way to proceed, no way to get there from here. Science fiction deals, or should deal, with *change;* and change, with all its subtle causes and consequences, is a thing that's seldom dealt with in mainstream fiction, which usually presupposes an eternal and unchanging present, which usually assumes that people and the lives they lead are pretty much the same down through the ages, that motives and passions and goals and desires and fears are interchangeable from generation to generation.

But that simply is not true. The present is neither eternal nor unchanging. Human society is a process, ever in motion; it is coming from somewhere, it is going someplace else. It was not the same then as now, nor will it ever be so again. We are not our parents; our children will not be us. The past was not 1970 with horses; the future will not be 1970 with chrome. THINGS CHANGE!

Everything changes: this is the central philosophic vision of good science fiction; if you cannot adjust to it, cannot believe it, cannot *feel* it and see it in everything around you and in yourself, then you're wasting your time trying to write the stuff.

Nothing is simple. Everything changes. Things connect.

You are what you eat.

And want, and do, and think, and fear, and dream.

You live in an organic surround, an interlocking and interdependent gestalt made up of thousands of factors and combinations thereof: cultural, technological, biological, psychological, historical, environmental. For all practical purposes, you *are* that surround; if the things that make up that surround are altered, then you will alter with them.

This is why imagination, although it's vital, is not by itself enough. One must have the vision to see the connections, and the sense to make them consistent. Much science fiction has failed on these grounds. Jules Verne predicted much of our present technology, but described it as working with a Victorian economy and society without working any change on that society *at all;* as a result, he is much less germane today than Wells, who knew better. If everything connects, then no social change, no technological innovation, takes place in tidy isolation.

Fictionally, this means that one postulate will spawn a host of others. If you have a world where everyone teleports, you can't have massive traffic jams; if everyone's a telepath, no one needs telephones; if everyone's part of a Group Mind, no one needs separate bedrooms. If all are blind, why do they need neon signs? If all have blasters, why do they need swords? If no one uses swords, where did the swords come from?

Alfred Bester, in *The Stars My Destination,* postulates that teleportation is a common ability — and the social ramifications of that one fact are endless: if you can teleport, and you don't like it where you are, why stay? Why live in cities at all? Why suffer night when you can follow the sun around the world? Why endure cold when you can teleport to the tropics? Why work when you can teleport to the scene of a natural disaster and loot and get away before the police catch you? And if the police do catch you, how are they going to hang on to you if you can teleport out of prison? What happens to the entertainment business when anyone can go anywhere? How do you keep a teleporting burglar out of your house? And in *The Demolished Man,* Bester does the same with telepathy: how can you keep a secret, get away with sharp business practices, lie, commit murder. The factors must add up, and the books must be balanced.

If you are writing about a near-future society, you must be careful of what Arthur C. Clarke has called a "failure of nerves" in prediction. Often a writer will present as a daringly possible innovation something that has already been developed and is in use; or worse, depict an advanced society that is less technologically sophisticated than the present. You are in trouble if your fictional tomorrow is already yesterday. One perfectly awful example of this was the slush pile story wherein the myopic women of the future had to choose between wearing "ugly eyeglasses" or "stumbling nearsighted through life" — it's the twenty-first century, and they haven't even heard of contact lenses! Conversely, it isn't enough to let your imagination run wild — you must not contradict what is presently known to be known unless you can explain why, and unless your explanation is plausible enough to suspend belief at least while the story is being read. The books must balance.

To write good SF, then, you must learn to perceive the hidden relationships that most do not; to pinpoint the trends just emerging in the present that might become prominent in the future, and to extrapolate logically their results in fictional terms, in terms of what they mean to *people.*

For practice, examine our own society and try to see it as a time traveler or a Martian might. It has come from somewhere, it is going somewhere else. There is a reason for everything, and a history behind every reason, right down to the design of the chairs on which you sit. Do you live in an apartment house? If so, then it's possible the building originally was a private house later cut up into apartments, and *that* explains the odd angle of the living room wall, or the blank window in the hall, or why you have to walk through what is now the bedroom to get to the bathroom. Slums turn into high-society districts, then back into slums. A hundred years ago, the street where you live might have been a swamp; a hundred years from now, it might be a swamp again, or a radioactive crater, or the lowest level in a two-mile-high city, or preserved in Lucite as a memorial to the quaint glories of the past.

And these are just the details of your physical environment. There are countless more, affecting the way you act and think and talk and dress and eat, who you think you are and how you feel about it. The world only seems static because we are too short-lived to see it change. If we could speed up time, condense eons into seconds, we would see mountains flow like water and fish learn to walk.

So your fictional future must be at least as complex as the present, or give the impression that it is. Practically speaking, you'll probably use only a relatively small percentage of these details in any one story — after all, your characters will not come in contact with *everything* — but you must still work the other details out; they must still be present in potential, or you will constantly stumble over contradictions and mistakes. Even if the reader never has occasion to learn in the course of a story that the city was overrun by the Vandarians two decades ago and that everyone paints himself blue on Sunday as a consequence, still the *author* must know that they do, and *the characters in the story must know it, too.* Your society should be worked out in detail and depth, in wonders and warts, monuments and pay toilets. If you thump it, it must ring sound, not hollow.

Play Your Wild Cards

Remember: the most important changes are not always the biggest or the most obvious. For example, one current theory blames much of the worldwide postwar population explosion on the adoption by backward villages of "technologies" such as the separation of well and latrine, and the use of wire mesh for doors and windows — things that drastically dropped the infant mortality rate. Much of the confusion in this area comes from a misunderstanding of what technology is, what society is, and how they affect us. Is technology a computer or a condom, a hydrogen bomb or a flint ax, a rocketship or a fliptop can? Does it affect your life more by putting you out of work through automation, or by killing the mosquitoes in the marsh behind your house, or by poisoning the air, or by providing you with eyeglasses if you are myopic? Is society the Gutenberg Bible or a nudity taboo, the jury system or the Eleusinian mysteries?

Remember that science fiction depicts not only new technologies and societal trends and their effects, but also how they cause people to react *to each other.*

Be careful with emotional emphasis, with how your characters *feel* about the things making up their lives. Even if their everyday appurtenances would to us be wondrous beyond belief, to them they would be mundane. This is a detail commonly gotten wrong in much SF, especially in some of the stories of the thirties and forties which tended to become worshipful hymns to the wonders of future technology. We don't sit in awe of our television sets, after all, even though in some ways their effect on us has been much more profound than the early prognosticators ever imagined. Conversely, what is commonplace to us may someday seem remarkable and romantic to our remote descendents. Robert Heinlein, Larry Niven and others have postulated that the people of the future, used to spaceships and supersonic shuttles, will nevertheless be aghast to think of the ordinary commuter of today going to work in the family car — no radar, no ballistic computer, no gyrostabilizers, no regulated traffic pattern; everything done by muscle power and guesswork. Who would ever dare to trade places with him? James Tiptree, Jr. has a beautiful story bit in which a highly advanced alien is staggering around the rush-hour traffic in Washington, D.C., taking deep breaths of the smog and saying things like "how primal. How unspoiled. Such peace!" It all depends on your context.

Be aware that wild factors can upset the most impeccably logical timetables. Hardly anyone foresaw the incredible acceleration of technological advance since WWII, or the mass cultural/psychological nervous breakdown of the late sixties. If your fictional scenario is exceedingly neat and tidy, perhaps you'd better throw in some wild factors, mess it up a little, make it more like the confusion in which we usually live.

If you are imagining a world that has degenerated into

barbarism, that world must still be self-consistent, and cultural cause-and-effect must still hold true. If you have no electricity, you have no electric lights; no needle and thread, you cannot sew; no plows, you cannot turn the ground.

Remember that our descendents won't be in chrome helmets and plastic tights — the working out of that proposition has produced some of the most worthwhile SF ever. The people who populate the worlds of Jack Vance, Ursula K. Le Guin, Robert Silverberg, Samuel R. Delany, Gene Wolfe, Joanna Russ, Philip K. Dick, Brain Aldiss, Damon Knight, Kate Wilhelm, Frederik Pohl and many others, are creatures of their own times, formed by those times in thought and spirit and habit. Isaac Asimov's people in *The Caves of Steel*, who so suffer from agoraphobia that they never leave their enclosed cities or see the sun; the Urbmon dwellers of Robert Silverberg's *The World Inside*, who have not only learned to live with conditions of extreme overcrowding, but who have come to find them desirable and spiritually satisfying; Jack Vance's Sirenese, who never show their naked faces from birth to death — who indicate their status by the type of mask they wear, and communicate with each other by playing appropriate passages on a bewildering variety of musical instruments. These are not familiar people, people we know. They are different kinds of people, and when we meet them we feel the shock of recognition — part fear, part amazement, part joy.

And like all literature, science fiction should entertain as well as enlighten. The most profound Heavy Thinking, the most intricate preplanning, the most germane social criticism, is useless and untenable if you have no story to tell, and no real people to tell it about.

The Problem With Powerpacks

One of your major narrative problems will be to get across to the reader an enormous amount of background material without gumming up the story's flow. There are as many solutions to this particular problem as there are writers. Some prefer to explain little or nothing directly — to tell the story as if it had been written by someone in the future for his contemporaries — and let the reader sort things out by implication and from context. One of the best examples of this technique is *Murder in Millennium VI,* by Curme Gray, a book that actually fulfills an ideal most writers only give lip service to: it explains *none* of the highly-complicated far future background — the reader must figure out or intuit what is happening page by page, on the fly, or he's lost. Similarly, many new writers like Felix Gotschalk also delight in plunging right into a story at full speed — "Who would have ever thought that men could alter the speed of the earth — and by such an obvious method as reverse photosynthesis?" — and letting the reader catch up if he can. James Tiptree, Jr. has said his preferred narrative technique is to "Start from the end and preferably 5,000 feet underground on a dark day and then DON'T TELL THEM." Many authors have achieved some remarkably successful results and striking effects in using this technique, but of course the danger here is that the writer will give the reader so little to go on that the reader will give up in bafflement. *Murder In Millennium VI,* for instance, is about as accessible and pellucid as a brick, and as a result it was not much of a commercial success.

One of the popular techniques is to introduce an outsider into your society as an observer, who will then learn about the society as the story progresses; the reader will learn also through his eyes (cf. *When the Sleeper Awakes* and *The Left Hand of Darkness*). Its major drawback is the plausibility of the observer — sometimes he tends to be something of a rabbit-out-of-a-hat, popping up out of nowhere with only the most tenuous of justifications.

Or you can couch the story as a fictionalized historical analysis from a viewpoint of a future *ahead* of the story's time; or, in a variant, write your story as an open-ended testament or memoir addressed to an unknown future audience, by an isolated survivor of an atomic war, for instance. Either of these approaches justifies the narrator's explanation of much that *his* audience wouldn't know (as well as *yours*) either directly in the narration or through "scholarly" footnotes, interpolations, introductions, afterwards, appendices. But this tends to make your story dry and talky, so encrusted with pseudoscholarly baggage that it has trouble moving.

Or the material can be conveyed through the omniscient author technique, or through interrelations of characters, or in any of a half-dozen other ways. You will learn in time which is best for you, how much to tell, how much to imply, how much to conceal — or you may make up a new technique. It may be a technical bottleneck at first, but you must at all costs resist the temptation to break through it by having your characters explain at length to each other things they should logically already know: "As you know, Frank, we are all androids, and must recharge our powerpacks every four hours or die . . . ." *That's probably the most common beginner's mistake on the books.*

Be careful with language, both in dialogue and in narration. Alexei Panshin says, "The future equivalent of 'damn,' expressed in present terms, is 'damn.' " But at the same time, it cannot be denied that many authors have had a great deal of success in working future slang and "alien" technology believably into their stories. Clearly, however, this isn't a knack every writer has, not even every writer of talent, and you must be clearheaded and ruthless in your appraisal of whether you possess it or not. You can't afford to fool yourself, or you will wreck the mood and believability of your stories again and again with language that sounds wrong or even ludicrous. You may even end up writing what James Blish has labeled "Call a rabbit a smeerp" stories: "They *look* like rabbits, but if you call them smeerps, that makes it science fiction."

Beware of the Star Trek Syndrome: creating stories that are unabashed duplicates of the Roman Empire and Nazi Germany. This is another prime example of mental laziness, since such societies are untenable on at least two grounds: one, that in spite of the time-honored proverb, history does *not* repeat itself, not in cozy one-to-one analogues anyway; and two, that such societies are drawn not from historically accurate sources, but from grossly distorted popular simplifications. The Roman Empire was vastly more complex, contradictory, surprising and multifaceted than the simplistic version we get from television, movies, and bad historical novels. And the people who inhabited it were as different from us as any citizens of A.D. 2100 are likely to be. In fact, the Old Egyptians and the Old Romans would be more alien to us than most authors' Martians.

Finally, remember that there is no such thing as THE future, only many different possible futures.

Shape of Stories to Come

Science fiction is not easy to write. It is often beyond the capabilities even of authors of talent and intelligence, because those qualities are not enough unless they are combined with a certain kind of imagination, perception and mental flexibility. So think it over. Appraise yourself carefully and with scrupulous self-honesty. You might not be capable of writing good science fiction, and if so, face up to it.

If, however, this is what you really want to write, and you feel at least potentially capable of meeting the special challenges it presents, then take heart: the task is not as impossible as it may appear. Few professional science fiction writers are geniuses, after all, and yet most have managed to cope. The biggest hurdle is the already-discussed psychological reorientation. After that, after you have trained your mind and your hands to the task, it is mostly a straightforward matter of learning your craft — and like any craft, it becomes easier with practice.

There are a few things you can do to make it more likely that you will succeed: first, and perhaps most important, if you are going to try to write science fiction, then for God's sake, READ it. Get an idea of what the present State of the Art is, of which magazines and anthologies are buying what. Another advantage of actively reading SF is that you'll save yourself a great deal of time and anguish on the road to becoming a selling writer. How? Because you will know better — you'll know *beforehand* that such-and-such is a worn-out cliché. And most of all: *if you don't enjoy reading science fiction, you're wasting your time trying to write it.*

Have as many inputs and interests as possible: most SF writers read copiously and catholically, and this greatly enriches their work. Anything and everything can be grist for your mill: science, anthropology, psychology, poetry, mythology. You need a good, working layman's knowledge of what's presently considered technologically possible or impossible, and at least a vague idea of why. There are many good popular science books available — some written by SF writers: Isaac Asimov, Arthur C. Clarke, Ben Bova — and you'll find that many experts, both scientists and teachers, are willing to assist you with advice and information if you're polite in asking for it. You'll also need to keep up with the constant flow of new ideas, so subscribe to some of the less technical scientific journals, like *Science News* and *Scientific American.*

Another helpful hint: science fiction is a friendly field. Established authors will frequently be willing to share their expertise with you, give you tips, point out pitfalls; genre editors are often willing to work extensively with you to renovate your story, sometimes spending much more time on it than is commercially justifiable.

And if none of the above lessens your trepidation, consider

this: there is a joy to this business of creating worlds that eventually almost becomes its own reward.

Try it now. Try out your new legs, and see how well you walk. Think yourself into the future, your future world. Think yourself into the skin of someone who lives there, and look around through his eyes. Remember to examine what it is you see with suspicion; sniff it carefully to see if it fits. Well, then, what *do* you see from the window in this world of the future? Do you see slender but sky-scraping Fäerie towers, elevated roadways winding among the building tops, clouds of small family helicopters drifting from one landing platform to another?

The hell you do! That's a 1940 version of 1970, remembered by a thousand paperback covers — as a vision of 2100, it's as inappropriate as a windmill in Times Square. You're not tapping anything worthwhile, you're still accepting easy answers, if that's what you see from your window. For that matter, should there be a window? In 2100? Suppose you're living in a plug-in modular apartment, close to the core, or in an inflatable rubber pyramid, or in a clear plastic fishbowl house, or 20 stories underground — would you have a window? a TV repeater screen? a hologram tank? a moving 3-D mural? a pornographic picture? a blank wall? What? What do *you* see there?

Now turn and look into your mirror (mirror?), there in the future. Are you a human being, a cyborg, an artificial brain-body environment, a mobile extensor for a computer, a chimera, or a mutated chimpanzee? Are you man, woman, hermaphrodite, neuter? Do you have extra limbs, organs, senses? Do you dye your skin? Have phosphorescent inlays of bone and jewels? Aesthetically-arranged patterns of multiple eyes? Do you have a morbid fear of ceilings? Are you sexually aroused by the color orange? Are you a devout Robbinsite? Is your building heated by fusion, by solar screens, by power broadcast from a black hole? Do you work as a plastic-eater, neurosis peddler, an algae-skimmer? Do you work? Do you go to the gene-reel for recreation, or are you one of those who believe that a self-inflicted lobotomy is the highest form of sensuality?

Professor J.B.S. Haldane once said: "The Universe is not only queerer than we imagine – it is queerer than we *can* imagine."

Nevertheless, we must try. To write good science fiction, we must make the attempt somehow to reason and intuit our way to a vision that is at least somewhat as complex as reality. We shall fail, inevitably, but perhaps in time we shall learn how to fail somewhat less totally.

And meanwhile, it's fun to try.

Yet another common error among new and unschooled science fiction writers is in the handling of politics in some far distant (or even relatively near) future. Here, the new writer fails to realize that no matter what his theme or subject matter, politics seen or unseen is a driving force behind his characters' behavior. To eliminate this deficiency, this article will open to the writer the somewhat mysterious and oftentimes complicated machinery of politics and government, with the aim of assisting you in creating a well-rounded future as well as a believable one.

Tom Purdom, *a past SFWA officer and newly elected Eastern Regional Director, is the author of several stories and books over the past decades, including the classic Reduction in Arms, a volume highly recommended to any aspiring SF author.*

CHAPTER 8:

Who's Going to Run Things in Twenty Three Hundred? And How Are They Going to Do It?

by
Tom Purdom

When some outraged citizens try to block a highway project because they think it's going to destroy their neighborhood, they are struggling with a political issue that couldn't arise in a nontechnological society. Most of our pollution and environmental problems wouldn't be bothering us if nobody had ever invented the automobile and the rest of modern industry. Even our American racial problem would probably be much less troublesome if modern technology hadn't thrown a lot of new obstacles in front of black Americans. Look at the political issues that are disturbing our society — overpopulation, the danger of thermonuclear war, the great gap between the rich nations of the Northern Hemisphere and the poor nations of the South — and you will find they have been heavily influenced by the nonpoliticians in agriculture, medicine and engineering. Science and technology are the primary sources of social change in our world, and they are probably going to have an even bigger impact on the society of the future. Pick up any issue of *Science News* or *Scientific American* and you will find the origins of some political conflict that may make our descendants run through the streets screaming with passion. A piece of genetic research that seems innocuous to the casual reader may someday lead to techniques that will double or triple the IQs of certain children and create a new division in society. A new discovery in astronomy may be the first mention of something that could cause an interstellar war centuries from now.

Science fiction is a natural field for the fiction writer who is interested in politics. Many science fiction writers write stories that can be called "political fiction" just as easily as they can be called "science fiction." Many mainstream political writers turn out books such as *Seven Days in May* and *Fail-Safe* that are certainly at least borderline science fiction. Even completely apolitical SF writers usually find themselves writing about politicians and government officials sooner or later. The real subject of science fiction, after all, isn't technology or science, but the potential problems of the future — some of which are bound to revolve around political issues.

The future is an inexhaustible source of novel, unhackneyed conflicts. If you like stories with strong, well-made plots — as I do — you're probably missing some very good story ideas if you aren't thinking about the political conflicts that may crop up in the decades and centuries to come.

You can't use all the wealth of possibilities science fiction offers you, however, if you don't understand SF and its audience. Science fiction is full of traps for the new writer, and political science fiction is no exception.

At the height of the Watergate scandal, many SF editors were flooded with "science fiction" stories that were merely thinly disguised versions of Watergate set in the future. Such borrowing may be all right when you're writing SF aimed at the mass audience, but you have to work a bit harder if you want to capture the regular science fiction reader. The more sophisticated SF readers know the problems of the future are going to be very different from the problems of the present, and they assume their writers know this, too. You can't take a current political situation, transplant it into the future with a few changes, and sell it to a science fiction editor who knows what he's doing.

It's also usually a mistake to write stories that merely extend a current trend into the future – unless that trend hasn't been done to death, or unless the author has a striking variation on a hackneyed subject. By now, however, the hard-working science fiction writers of the world have rung hundreds of changes on overpopulation, urban violence, nuclear war, pollution, and all the more obvious trends. Some writers can still find gold in those particular hills, but I usually feel more confident when I'm exploring regions other people have ignored. If I notice that some SF writers are writing stories in which the United States is convulsed by an apocalyptic race war (as they were a few years ago), I can usually find something else to get excited about.

The Problems of Solutions

Many people make a distinction between "character oriented" science fiction and "technologically oriented" SF, but I've always thought that was a dangerous way to classify SF stories if you're actually trying to write the stuff. We've all read science fiction stories that merely present an idea or describe a new gadget, but they aren't the stories that have the most impact on readers, and they aren't *real* stories, either, in my opinion. A real story has to be about people; it usually has to have a strong conflict, too — and some of the most challenging conflicts human beings will ever face are being created by the advance of science.

In other words, don't stick your nose in the air, and decide you don't have to know anything about science because you're one of those super-humane types who's interested in *people.* Read every science book you can find time to read. Start with children's books if you don't know anything about a certain branch of science, and the books for grownups don't make sense to you. Read magazines like *Science News, Psychology Today, Natural History, Medical World News, The Futurist.* Talk to scientists and engineers. Sooner or later, if you get enough information in your head, something will suggest a conflict that would make a good story. The back of your neck will start tingling, ideas will start jumping around in your mind, and you'll know you've hooked something that will be worth all the effort you can bring to it.

In addition to that kind of random exploring (which is fun in itself, of course, or I. probably couldn't make myself do it), I also like to look at current problems that interest me, and think about the conflicts that could be created by some of the possible *solutions.* Too many political writers seem to think history will stop once their particular political program goes into effect. Science fiction writers should go one step further and recognize that today's solutions are often tomorrow's problems. Many of our current environmental problems, for example, spring from developments such as DDT, that were supported by people who wanted to do something about disease and malnutrition. The Founding Fathers came up with some interesting solutions to the problems of free government when they wrote our Constitution, but we have now spent nearly 200 years trying to make their solutions work — and few people would claim that those two centuries have been completely free of conflict and trouble.

My novel *Reduction in Arms* grew out of my own interest in the arms race, but it isn't about a thermonuclear war. The basic assumption of the book is one of the possible solutions to the problem — a treaty that limits all military forces and prohibits secret research. Once you have such a treaty, obviously, it has to be inspected and enforced. And the novel focuses on the problems of the people who have to cope with that particular chore.

Robert Silverberg's novella "Going" is an especially fine example of a story that could have been written through this approach. In a society in which natural death has been eliminated, one solution to the problem of overpopulation would be voluntary euthanasia. But how would you feel if you had to choose the moment of your own death? When you eliminate natural death, you eliminate one pressure on the individual, but you replace it with another.

I also like to pick up standard science fiction situations now and then and see what I can do with them. I use a technique I once came across in an article by a mystery writer: I ask myself a lot of questions about the basic situation, and try to come up with the most interesting and imaginative answers possible.

When I wrote my SF action novel *Five Against Arlane,* for example, I was working with one of the most overused plot situations in the field: a revolt against a tyrannical government. So I asked myself questions about every aspect of the story I could think of, and tried to work out answers that would help me overcome the fact that readers have seen this situation dozens of times (hundreds, probably, if they're the kind of people who read every SF book published). What made the dictator seize control of his planet? How is this planet different from all of the other planets SF readers have read about? What kind of weapons do the characters use? What factors in their environment will give them attitudes and feelings that will make them seem like people of the future instead of transplanted present-day Americans? When the basic situation is very familiar, every detail in the story must be as original as possible.

Human Limits

Once you have a basic conflict, you still have to develop a story line. And here, too, there is a big, obvious trap you should avoid if you're trying to write reasonably believable fiction. Don't try to feed your readers a story in which the hero does far more than one human being can be expected to do.

At one point in the recent past, science fiction readers were being buried under an avalanche of novels in which the hero would join an underground movement that was supposed to overthrow some terrible future government and bring society back to good old Twentieth Century Americanism. The underground would overthrow the thought controllers (admen/geneticists/religious fanatics), and all the people who had been enslaved by the evil government would immediately become good, right-thinking, civic-minded free citizens.

In real life, of course, important social changes are rarely brought about by one person, and revolutions rarely have such simple-minded happy endings. The process that brought on the French Revolution took at least a generation and involved hundreds of writers, agitators and politicians — and the end result of all that effort was the Napoleonic Empire, not liberty. Political change is a diffused, drawn-out process that usually involves masses of people and rarely ends exactly as the planners had hoped. If you want to keep your readers turning the pages because they're totally involved in the fate of your characters, you have to people your stories with characters who have some of the limitations of real human beings.

This doesn't mean, of course, that your characters have to be weak, helpless victims. For one thing, you can always place your hero at a strategic point where the actions of one person really can affect history. I sometimes like to call this the *For Whom the Bell Tolls* approach. In Ernest Hemingway's novel, Robert Jordan and his band of guerrillas are supposed to blow up one bridge — a reasonable objective for a few people. If Jordan can destroy the bridge at the right time, however, his actions will have a decisive effect on a much larger situation. The Fascist army will be thrown into confusion when it tries to bring up reinforcements and stop an attack by the Spanish Republican army, and the Republicans may win the battle — and if the Republican army wins the battle, it may stop Fascism in Spain and thereby stop its advance all over Europe. As Carlos Baker points out in his book *Hemingway: the Writer as Artist,* Jordan is at the center of a group of concentric circles that eventually include the entire world.

Science fiction is a particularly good form for people who like to write this kind of story. Real situations in which individuals can play a crucial role are naturally rare in real life. In a science fiction story, however, you can manipulate the whole future of the human race, and it isn't hard to come up with believable situations in which a few individuals can have a major effect on their society.

Start With the Human Heart

You can also take the opposite approach and write stories in which the basic political situation is treated as an unalterable reality, about which the characters can do nothing. This type of story can be extremely realistic, and it can have just as much action and suspense as a story in which the characters try to make vast, sweeping changes in their society.

In Aleksandr Solzhenitsyn's novel *The First Circle,* for example, all of the characters are affected by Stalin's tyranny, but none of them can do anything to end it. Stalin's dictatorship is an unalterable fact of life, like a hurricane or an earthquake; nobody forms an underground and tries to overthrow the Man of Steel and his cohorts. Solzhenitsyn's characters aren't passive vegetables, however. They all make some response to Stalin's domination of Russian society. Some acquiesce to it, some profit by it, some defy it. There are heroes and cowards, lovers and rebels, and the story generates a tremendous amount of suspense as it approaches its conclusion. But no one ever suggests any of the characters can actually end the tyranny that is causing all of their problems.

Harry Harrison's *Make Room, Make Room* is a good example of a science fiction novel with this kind of plot. All of the characters in Harrison's novel have to cope with the overpopulation of New York, but none of them can do anything that will change the basic situation. Nobody hands out birth control leaflets on the streets; nobody forms a secret underground organization and tries to slip birth control pills into the water supply. Instead, Harrison shows us a small group of people coping with the day-to-day problems caused by overpopulation. A policeman has to deal with riots caused by shortages of food and water. People fight over living space and the losers have to hunt for homes in abandoned cars. The policeman's girlfriend has to choose between her affection for him and her desire for the meat substitutes, private living quarters, and other "luxuries" a criminal can provide.

This type of situation can be used in action fiction, too. In one of my short stories, the conflict arises out of the fact that even poor people have lots of powerful, potentially deadly playthings in the very rich society of the twenty-first century. The hero can't change this unpleasant social situation; it never occurs to him that he can. He is a cop who has to deal with the problem in the normal course of his work. He restores the peace when a bunch of kids get violent, and then goes on to his next assignment, just as a contemporary cop tickets a speeder and then goes after the next one.

Whatever you do, always remember that at the center of every good story there is always a human being who is involved in an emotional situation that is so fundamental and widespread that almost any reader can identify with him. The great eighteenth century French general, Maurice de Saxe, once wrote that "the human heart is the starting point in all matters pertaining to war." That's just as true of politics and even truer of writing political fiction. People read fiction because they want to read about people and events, not because they're interested in your political opinions. We don't read *The First Circle* and *For Whom the Bell Tolls* because Solzhenitsyn hates tyranny and Hemingway thought Spain should be governed by the Spanish Republicans instead of the Spanish Fascists; we read them because they tell us about people caught up in dictatorship or war, and make us feel some of the things those people feel. That is the basic and most important task of the fiction writer — and it's particularly easy to forget, unfortunately, when you're writing about politics.

Ursula K. Le Guin's novel *The Dispossessed* is one of the finest political novels anyone has written inside or outside of science fiction in the last decade. Le Guin describes two different political and economic systems in the course of her Nebula Award-winning novel, and you can treat her book, if you want to, as a treatise on the merits of two different social systems. To me, however, *The Dispossessed* is essentially the story of a creative, conscientious individual who discovers he can't live a satisfying, moral life in any society that has been shaped by the realities of human nature. This is a dilemma as old as the human conscience, and Shevek's attempts to deal with it make a moving, suspenseful story that is far more significant than any debate about the merits of anarchism and capitalism.

When you write fiction, you should never forget you are creating an experience, not a pamphlet. The fiction writer doesn't write about political issues. He writes about people who are involved in political situations.

"If I were told that I could write a novel in which I could indisputably establish as true my point of view on all social questions," Tolstoy once wrote a friend, "I would not dedicate two hours to such a work; but if I were told that what I wrote would be read 20 years from now by those who are children today, and that they would weep and laugh over it and fall in love with the life in it, then I would dedicate all my existence and all my powers to it."

The last time I looked at a paperback bookstore, *War and Peace* was still sitting in the racks. So were a lot of science fiction novels that were written 20 and 25 years ago. And people who hadn't even been born when those SF novels were written were buying them and falling in love with the life in them. Don't you wish you had written some of those novels? Doesn't that seem a more attractive ambition than writing a book that proves you have the only proper attitude toward the price of sugar or the size of the American defense budget?

Making It Seem Real

Fiction writing is largely an art of detail. The writer achieves his effects by presenting his readers with one detail after another — events, characters, lines of dialogue, bits of background. The reader perceives the story one detail at a time and keeps on reading, partly because the details interest him. If your details are good, then your characters and your background will seem real and people may be interested in your story; if they're dull and unimaginative, very few people will read past the first five pages and everything else you have to offer will probably be wasted.

My friend Richard E. Peck once wrote a story in which

the Earth was visited by aliens who lived underwater on their home planet and traveled in a water-filled spaceship. For this one short story, he made up a list of fifty ways in which a water-filled spaceship would be different from a human ship. He only used a few of those details in his story, but his preliminary work undoubtedly gave the story weight and credibility.

Nobody can tell you how to make up all the details that make an imaginary situation seem believable. That's one of the things you're paid to do. I do have a few general principles, however, that I try to keep in mind when I'm creating a fictional political situation, and some of them may be useful to other writers.

To begin with, it helps to have your head stocked with information about real politicians and real political situations. Read histories, biographies, memoirs, letters. Eat up books like *An American Melodrama: The Presidential Campaign of 1968* and Theodore White's *Making of the President* series. Go to rallies and meetings where you can see political figures in the flesh and note their personal mannerisms and the way they handle audiences. Watch how the photographers pop up, right on cue, when the police commissioner puts out his fist and strikes a fighting pose. Note how a certain local politician holds his head as if it were being bathed in floodlights and he were constantly trying to get the light at just the right angle.

There is no substitute, in my opinion, for actual involvement in political campaigns. Every writer should do this at least once or twice. Every political writer should do it as often as possible. I've been a division worker and poll watcher in most of the primary and general elections that have been held in Philadelphia during the last 15 years, and as far as I'm concerned, I've never lost an election; my candidates have lost (frequently), but I've always learned things that I could put to use sooner or later.

Poll watching and ward-level politics may seem like a poor way to understand the minds of presidents and senators, but you haven't really learned anything about the political system until you've worked in a primary election on election day and locked horns with a good committeeman from one of the regular party organizations. Get up at five in the morning so that you can get to the polls early and make sure the committeeman doesn't misread the numbers on the voting machines. Stay on your feet all day. Watch how the committeeman gets the voters to vote his way. Fight with him when he tries to go into the voting booth with a voter. Try to tell an average voter how to split his ticket or perform some other complicated, highly skilled task. Sit on the curb with the committeeman near the end of a 14-hour day and chat with him in the unguarded way people talk when they're tired. Stand over his shoulder when the votes are read off the machine and make sure he doesn't make a few well-placed errors in the count. It is an educational opportunity that is available, free, to all citizens of our republic, and you are missing a great deal if you don't take advantage of it.

I also find it helpful to remember there is usually a significant difference between a political system as it is described by its supporters, and the system as it really is. If you can get some of this dissonance between theory and reality into your story, it's going to seem that much more real to your readers. The people who really have power, for example, may not be the people who are supposed to have it in theory. In medieval Europe, the kings of France and England were supposed to be at the top of the heap in their respective countries; in practice, the people who really had the most power were the stronger barons and dukes, and they in their turn were constantly warring with underlings who didn't always obey orders and bend the knee like loyal feudal vassals were supposed to. Power flowed up and down in complex patterns that didn't look anything like the neat lines on an organizational chart.

Similarly, some of the most powerful people in a modern U.S. government may be legislators who have managed to work their way onto obscure committees that give them a huge, unheralded influence over the legislative process. Or a bureaucrat may become so powerful (like the late J. Edgar Hoover) that his nominal superiors have to deal with him as if they were negotiating with a foreign country. Or middle-level technical experts may possess specialized knowledge and skills that give them the power to disrupt a whole social system, as in SF stories like Katherine MacLean's "The Missing Man" or Robert Heinlein's "The Roads Must Roll."

Most political systems are also set up to favor those who are already in power. There are a lot of ways this can be done, and you can add to the verisimilitude of your work by studying a few of them.

Gerrymandering is one of the better known techniques for doing this, but there are other methods that are less obvious. In my own city of Philadelphia, for example, the courts at the lowest level of the judiciary system are presided over by judges who are called magistrates. Each magistrate presides over a court in a particular neighborhood of the city, but he isn't elected by the people in his neighborhood. Every magistrate runs "at large"; everybody in the city votes for all 28 magistrates.

That may seem like a minor oddity in our election laws, but it means, in effect, that all 28 magistrates are essentially political appointees. If each magistrate were elected by the voters in his own district, an independent candidate might run in a primary now and then and beat the candidate put up by one of the regular party organizations; many people can achieve a certain amount of renown in their own neighborhoods and put together an organization that can win an election in one area of the city. But very few people are so well-known that they can run in a city-wide election and overcome the city-wide "controlled vote" — the thousands and thousands of voters who come out on primary day and obediently push down the levers their committeemen tell them to push. Nobody ever runs for magistrate, therefore, without the support of one of the regular organizations, and the magistrates' jobs form one of the offices the parties use to reward their loyal workers.

Magistrates may seem like unimportant people compared to the glamorous national candidates who dominate the TV version of politics, but they are, in fact, very important to the professional politicians. Professional politicians don't think like ordinary citizens, and I try to keep that in mind, too, when I write about them.

Amateurs and semipros tend to be interested in issues and candidates. They come out and work in an election because they're concerned about air pollution or foreign policy, and they think a particular candidate will do something about their pet problem if he's elected. Professionals, on the other hand, tend to be careerists. They work hard in election after election so they can advance from job to job, just like corporation executives. They may be interested in a judgeship or some other job in their local government, or they may want to work their way up in the party structure. To the professionals, therefore, the big jobs that excite the amateurs may be far less important than the minor offices that are often ignored by the average voter. When a party leader looks at a potential candidate for the top of the ticket, he usually has one big question on his mind: will this guy bring out the voters and help me elect the rest of the ticket?

To the average voter, a political campaign is generally a contest between a few politicians who want to be senators, governors and presidents. Now and then it may even be a contest between candidates who have different ideas about various social problems. To the professionals, it's more like a struggle between two gangs, and the issues and the top-level candidates are just tools they use to win the election for their team.

Look out for the Great American Presidential Obsession when you write about future political situations in the United States. The modern Presidency is a peculiar office with a special place in our national mythology, and many Americans seem to think politics begins and ends with the superhero in the White House. Many SF writers seem to forget that our complex American political system includes all kinds of smaller political units — states, cities, counties, city council districts, police precincts, congressional districts, school districts, etc., etc., etc. A President can have a vague and indirect effect on 200 million people, but a local political boss can often have much more impact on the personal lives of the individuals in his territory. The struggles in smaller political units are usually much more suitable subjects for fiction, too, since they usually involve fewer people, and each individual's immediate future may be drastically affected by the outcome. See, for example, the mileage C. P. Snow gets out of a college faculty election in his novel *The Masters.* Or take a look at Alexei Panshin's *Rite of Passage* and Poul Anderson's *Tau Zero*, and see what a good writer can do with the inhabitants of a single starship.

Yearn to Learn

There's no substitute for direct experience if you want to write about politics, but there's no substitute for reading about other periods, either. You can't let yourself get wrapped up in the present if you're writing science fiction. Nixon and Haldeman and your local police commissioner are all worth studying, but so are Frederick the Great and Elizabeth I. The society of the twenty-third century probably won't be anything like our modern democracy, but we humans have tried so many different political systems in the past that it will probably look like *something* we've already lived with.

Certain kinds of political organization seem to crop up again and again. Julius Caesar, Mayor Daley, and Lorenzo de Medici all operated under different constitutions, but are they really that different? They are all political "bosses," and you can understand a lot about Daley if you study Lorenzo and Caesar — and vice versa.

You should learn everything you can, therefore, about the actual workings of feudalism, capitalism, hereditary aristocracies, monarchies, socialist states, the different kinds of republics and democracies, and all the other forms of government people have tried from time to time. Look at the cycles societies seem to go through. Think about the reasons different kinds of systems work in one era and don't work in another. Observe how writers like Poul Anderson and L. Sprague de Camp use different kinds of historical political systems in their stories. Notice how they manage to convey some of the facets of human behavior that seem to be timeless.

No system of government is ever exactly duplicated in another era, however. Don't do what a lot of science fiction writers have done and take the British Empire or European feudalism and transplant them bodily into the future with all their customs and trappings intact. Stories with that kind of background tend to seem thin and unbelievable. There's nothing wrong with a galactic empire if you like that kind of thing, but it isn't going to help your story if you don't make it seem like a unique, carefully thought-out personal vision.

Isaac Asimov's *The Stars Like Dust* contains a good example of the right way to develop a society that is based on a historical model. Asimov's novel takes place in a galactic empire that is ruled by hereditary aristocrats, but he doesn't fill his pages with counts, dukes and barons. Instead, he gives his rulers titles like the Rancher of Widemos and the Autarch of Lingane — and provides us with a little more evidence that we are looking at a *future* society, not a past society in which horses have been turned into spaceships and swords into rayguns.

Never forget, furthermore, that politics is inextricably intertwined with economics. I don't feel like I really know a character if I don't know how he makes his living, and I feel the same way about societies. Certain types of economic situations force certain types of political organization on people, and you can't build a convincing imaginary social system if you don't understand that. Our modern democracies would probably be impossible without our high level of affluence, mass education, mass communications, and many of the other changes industrialization has made in our societies. The armored knights of the age of chivalry were merely the upper classes of a vast agricultural society in which land was the basis of wealth; their whole society was based on the fact that it takes a certain number of acres to support a warrior on horseback, and they faded into the history books when capital and machinery became more important than acres of topsoil.

What will happen to our politics if we double or triple the standard of living in the rich nations of Europe and North America? How will international affairs be affected by the economic exploitation of the Solar System? What kind of political system will we develop when every college-educated family can arm itself with biological weapons that can devastate entire cities?

The best science fiction has always been written by writers who base their imaginings on a great deal of knowledge. You can't write it, in my opinion, if you don't really enjoy learning things. You'll never learn everything you need to know — but if you can learn even a small percentage of it, you'll do a much better job when you sit down at your typewriter and start turning your knowledge into the drama, tragedy and comedy that are the true subject of *all* fiction, whether it has an adjective in front of it or not.

A popular SF staple both in print and on the screen is the slime-dripping, multitentacled, myriad-faceted eyeballed Alien. He has been a walking carrot, a mutant tarantula, a "thing" from the nonexistent seas of Mars, and a dozen other personalities. Unfortunately, few of these aliens are, in fact, alien, and few were rationally considered before being filmed or published. This article should, if considered carefully, help you to avoid not only a weary editor's shake of the head, but also that dreaded rejection slip.

George R. R. Martin, *recently married, has been writing SF for several years and has been nominated for both Hugo and Nebula Awards on many occasions; his first win came in 1975 for the moving "A Song For Lya," a Hugo much deserved. His first book is a collection of stories from Avon, under the same title.*

CHAPTER 9:

First, Sew On a Tentacle (Recipes for Believable Aliens)
by
George R. R. Martin

Aliens.

Call them extraterrestrials or bug-eyed monsters. Call them nonhumans or imaginary beings or little green men. Call them anything you please. Under any name, they thrive and multiply. Aliens were part of SF long before Hugo Gernsback "fathered" the genre in 1926; since then, they have been one of its staples. Generations of SF writers sweating over their typewriters have filled the literature with more alien races than anyone could shake a stick at — and anyone who would *want* to shake a stick at some of them might be considered a bit strange himself.

The shapes of the alien are legion. There are aliens with tentacles and aliens with pincers and aliens with no limbs at all. There are aliens who fly and aliens who swim and a few aliens who roll about on wheels. Some aliens breathe oxygen, others breathe chlorine, some don't breathe at all. The permutations are endless.

After all this, the aspiring SF writer faces an imposing task when he sets out to create something new, the very latest word in aliens. But it can be done. The possibilities are endless, too, for the writer who works at it.

Yet the task is far from easy. Of all those aliens who have gone before — the vast slimy slithering flapping cackling mass of them — the majority are just Not Very Good. For a variety of different reasons. Nonetheless, memorable aliens *do* exist — proving that the problems can be overcome — and there is a wealth of information for the young writer in the famous failures as well.

In the face of the problems, however, a beginner would be quite justified in asking, "Why bother?" Especially today. Aliens tend to be featured less in contemporary SF than in the literature of the so-called "Golden Age" (although the modern creations are by and large better, as writers learn from earlier mistakes). In an age when SF is winning more and more literary respectability, more than one ambitious writer has locked his aliens in the closet. Writers are afraid to be seen in public with a green-skinned companion, lest a critic jump out of the bushes and shout "Pulp!" at them.

Are aliens worth doing, then? Or are they somehow tainted forever with the ink of gaudy four-color covers?

Well, the concept of the alien did enjoy a long and lusty youth in the SF pulps, and those adolescent extraterrestrials were immature and stupid and embarrassing as often as not, like adolescent SF itself. But the *idea* of the alien predates the genre pulps. H.G. Wells, certainly no pulp hack, created one of the greatest alien races: the Martians in *The War of the Worlds*. And before Wells, fantasy writers were filling their books with sundry sorts of imaginary beings, creatures very similar to today's alien in concept and intent and literary function, however different the trappings of the flesh might be.

Those writers who see in the shadowy figure of the alien nothing but a pulp convention are literarily blind; the alien is more than that, far more. The alien is a modern elf, a troll, a ghost. The alien is god and devil. The alien is mystery and color and romance. The alien is the ultimate outsider, and the outsider has been a concern of serious literature since before there *was* an animal called "serious literature."

Writers who purge aliens from their fiction (along with other pulp devices like spaceships and time travel) and try to write a more "mature" brand of SF only cripple themselves. For these devices, this array of symbols, and the authorial freedom that they represent, were the very things that gave emotional power to much of pulp SF, despite its always cardboard characters and often ghastly style. If modern SF has less tolerance for bad writing, this does not mean it has no room for aliens. Mature SF is not a literature without the alien; rather it is full of mature aliens, and one hopes they are done better than any in the past.

The alien is a creature of myth, a potent symbol, an ofttimes searing image. But mostly, for the writer, the alien is a tool, a story device that can be used in many different ways to make the author's statement clearer and stronger and more effective. And a good writer uses *all* of his tools.

For the aspiring author hungering after a first or second sale, there are more practical aspects as well. A good alien can help sell a story; the device has so much vitality, when done well, that it can sometimes cause an editor to overlook the flaws of an otherwise undistinguished chunk of prose. I sincerely wish that I had a nickel for each time I'd heard a remark along the lines of, "Well, his characters aren't interesting and his style is turgid and I can't say the plot made much sense, but I sure did like his aliens!" An interesting extraterrestrial has saved many a stinker from oblivion.

A badly done alien, of course, will save nothing. Editors see thousands of cardboard creepie-crawlies every year in the slush pile submissions that flood their offices. The skin shade and the number of tentacles may vary widely, but the creatures do have much in common — generally they are poorly conceived and ineptly handled, each one like all those before, displaying little thought and less strangeness. They are clichés, aliens only by authorial fiat; actually, they are human beings in funny suits, prancing about and trying to *look* like aliens, and failing.

To fashion a viable alien (or race of aliens) a writer must first learn at least the rudiments of creating a believable character; then, when those problems are out of the way, he can go on to face a whole new set. There is no simple formula. But there are some procedures that can be helpful (particularly to the neophyte), some rules worth following, and a good many common pitfalls to avoid.

A fan recently asked Howard Waldrop, a young Texas SF writer of immense talent, how he could go about learning to write science fiction. "Well," Waldrop told him, "the first thing is, you have to start reading it in 1952. . . ."

This is true of virtually *any* kind of writing (the writer who does not read what he's trying to write is a fool or a hopeless amateur), but it is particularly true in SF, where the demands are rather extraordinary and the premium on originality is high. Unless he has a fairly extensive grounding in the genre, a fledging SF writer is going to be doomed to a long apprenticeship of learning things the hard way, turning out one "original" story after another only to find that all of them have been done to death by people who were buried before s/he first set eyes on a typewriter. Waldrop's Rule is immediately relevant to a writer who wants to create a believable, memorable alien. He should first learn what a good alien looks, smells and sounds like. There are lessons in all of the stories I intend to cite, good examples and bad ones. So before you write, read. Then you can start to think about *your* aliens.

Funny Suits Do Not an Alien Make

The first thing you should think about is — why is this alien in my story?

An alien is first a character. Like any character in a work of fiction, it must have a role, a function, a litera   reason to exist within the framework of your tale. If you want to include an alien simply for the sake of creating an alien, then you've already made a fatal mistake. You're giving yourself additional writing problems you don't need, and you'll probably do grave damage to your story. One good rule to keep in mind: if your alien, for story purposes, could just as easily be a human, then *make* it a human. The writers who ignore this rather commonsense stipulation wind up with very unimpressive aliens; humans in funny suits again.

The rule has a broader application than it might seem to have at first glance. Most SF writers follow it somewhat; only a few take it to its logical conclusion, and apply it all the time. Those who do not, I think, are wrong. Their particular failing is in underestimating the mutability of humanity and human culture.

Most SF writers tend to use humans as their protagonists; these humans, in the vast majority of cases, are products of a Judeo-Christian, technological, Western culture. That is, *our* culture, or its offshoots, projected into the future. Oh, to be sure, writers extrapolate and make changes, but most build their humans on the same foundations, so that reader and writer and protagonist share many common concerns, beliefs, attitudes. These assumptions go unspoken, chiefly, but they are there.

No writer of any repute would try to foist off an alien race or culture that *also* had all this in common. Not deliberately, at any rate; our culture is so much a part of us that *every* writer has some of these attitudes seeping into even the best of his aliens. But the careful craftsman fights this tendency.

Quite often, however, otherwise conscientious artists will set their protagonist (this star child born of Western humanity) into a situation of conflict or counterpoint with an alien culture. Then, rolling merrily along, they proceed to model their "alien" culture on some variant of pretechnological or non-Western man, on the blithe assumption that this makes it inhuman.

Many of these stories sell. Many readers seem to enjoy them. Still, they are flawed; this is cheapjack craftmanship at best, and it will be less and less tolerated in the years to come, as SF's aliens grow more sophisticated. Dressing up a Cargo Cult, for example, in green skin and tentacles does *not* make it an alien society. It will wash only for uninformed readers who have never heard of Cargo Cults.

Stories of social and cultural conflict are very common in SF, of course. And that is good. These can be powerful, important stories, articulating problems and possibilities of our own culture and society (and human nature itself) by means of the challenge of other cultures and societies. SF can do this better than any other form of literature. To be sure, this is the stuff of human history, and can be considered within historical fiction as well. But in history, the important questions and the basic issues were often obscured by other factors that influenced the turn of events; personalities, chance, natural causes. Reformulated in the fictional context of SF, the conflicts between the ways men live can be seen more clearly.

But they are human conflicts. There is no need to cast them in the clothes of human versus alien. To expand on the original rule, then: if the only important differences between the aliens and the humans in your story are cultural and social, then your story ought not have aliens at all.

TV's *Star Trek* series provides a quite excellent example of what *not* to do, in the person of the pointy-eared Vulcan, Mr. Spock, perhaps the world's most famous alien. Not too great a distinction, since Spock is sadly quite a poor job. The creators of the series wanted cultural conflict; Spock is a man from a culture where emotions are taboo, where intellect is all, set in an environment where he is surrounded by normal emotional humans. The proper way to have done this would have been to make Spock a native of a world colonized by humans, of some particular sect or religion, and inculcated with that society's dislike of emotion.

Instead, they gave Spock pointed ears and made him an unemotional alien (instead of an unemotional man); the result was idiocy. Spock is a half-breed, we are told, child of a human-alien liaison. That's impossible, for starters; humans will *not* be interfertile with aliens. And Spock and his "alien" people depart less from the norms of Western humanity than any of a hundred cultures living now on Earth. The physical differences are so slight as to be meaningless. In short, the Vulcans are *lousy* aliens. They were not alone; *Star Trek* often specialized in lousy aliens, particularly during its last year.

The show took the concept of parallel evolution (the idea that aliens may evolve more or less along the same lines as humanity, independently, because the humanoid form is logical and optimal for an intelligent, tool-using animal) and drove it to ridiculous extremes, spewing forth one alien species after another that looked like humans (except for blue hair, or silver toenails, or ...), talked just like humans (from somewhere in history), thought just like humans, and so forth. One of the all-time low points in the creation of alien species came on the sorry night when *Star Trek* postulated an alien race that had evolved parallel to us to such an extent that they had independently written the Preamble to the US Constitution, word for word, as well as designing the American flag.

The same faults, in less grotesque form, can be found in much of written SF as well, where the author has used aliens who are exactly-like-humans instead of humans. The offenders even include some classic works, like Isaac Asimov's early short, "Nightfall." Asimov wrote the story based on an Emerson quotation dealing with what men would be like if they saw the stars only one night in a thousand years. He peopled his tale with aliens, but still could reply to Emerson, since his aliens are so much like Americans of the 1930s as to make the differences meaningless (their newspapermen even seem to have the same attitudes as those from 1935 B-movies). The story still works, since the power of the theme transcends the clumsiness, but the "aliens" are a hideous blemish.

There are, of course, many writers who do it right. The numerous works of Jack Vance are particularly worthy of study. Vance is a glorious decadent, perhaps the most colorful and imaginative writer now working in the genre, and his stories and novels — though full of kidnapping and shooting and derring-do and sundry high adventure — are virtually all tales of cultural conflict. He creates social systems with backhanded ease when lesser writers strain and sweat for years to get lesser and littler effects; his worlds and societies range from the mildly strange to the out-and-out bizarre to the downright kinky, with every stop in between. All of them are painted in loving, living detail; they are rich with color and custom and texture. Some are based on real historical cultures; some are based on nothing but the author's deranged brilliance.

And nearly every one of these societies is human.

Vance does not avoid aliens, of course. But he's smarter than most SF writers; he uses aliens only when the story needs them. When the only differences are social-and-cultural, he uses exotic humans.

As literary devices, aliens and exotic humans should not

be interchangeable, and Vance seems to know this, which accounts for much of his success in this regard. In his four-book Planet of Adventure series, for example, he creates no less than four alien races, each different in appearance and culture and psychology. Their societies are tilted and twisted just as wildly as the worlds of typical Vancian exotic humans, but for the aliens there is an added strangeness that Mr. Spock never possesses. A real sense of the alien; a Vulcan is human, his society is human, but a Dirdir or a Blue Chasch is — something else.

Ursula K. Le Guin is another author worthy of note, if only because of her masterpiece, *The Left Hand of Darkness.* The people of the world Winter have one critical physiological difference from ordinary humans; they are sexual neuters except during certain periods of "kemmer," when they can become either male or female. Thus each individual is both man and woman many times during life.

A small difference. But it is enough to make the Gethenians more unlike you and me than 99 percent of the awful papier-maché aliens who have plagued SF. A lesser writer would have made Winter an alien world, and destroyed the story. Le Guin, a thoughtful craftsman, made it a lost colony, and her people human.

The first important lesson in using aliens in SF is knowing when *not* to use them; the writers who have ignored this rule are the culprits who have produced most of the clichéd little green men of pulps past. Humans in funny suits.

The World-Builders

Let's say you passed the first test; your story does have a perfectly good reason to include an alien (and there are hundreds of perfectly good reasons), so now you have to design him/her/it. A lot of important decisions have to be made. What does the thing look like? How does it think? What sort of world does it come from? Does it have a culture, a society? What sort? How is it going to communicate with your human characters, assuming that you have human characters? How does it communicate with its fellow aliens, for that matter?

Questions, questions, questions; if you want to sell your story, you had damned well better have answers, answers, answers. And none of them arbitrary, because they're all related, and if they don't hang together under stress, the reader (or the editor) is going to start punching big nasty holes in your nice paper aliens.

It is *not* vital that you answer all these questions in your story. Some writers do, habitually, but for most it isn't a good idea, since a block of information that size can stop your action dead and turn the reader off (unless it itself is of immense intrinsic interest). Besides, the reader doesn't need all that information. You do. To make you think, to ensure that the things that do appear on paper are logical and consistent. A good alien society is like an iceberg; only the tip appears in the story. The rest is below surface, in your head and in your notes.

The process of creating an alien, the actual steps taken in fleshing out an imaginary being, vary widely from author to author. No two work exactly alike. The best alienologists, however, do seem to use one of two possible approaches to the problem. Both methods are worth discussing.

The first method is often called world-building. It is more than just a means of fashioning aliens, of course; it concerns itself with whole planets and ecosystems. But aliens are an important by-product of the process.

The world-builders often start without even a story idea, with nothing but a star of a certain type, a planet at a certain distance with an atmosphere made up of this-and-that in these amounts. From foundations like these, they work out an ecology to fit the particular conditions of each world, then imagine what sort of sentient being might emerge from such an ecology. Only after all this is established do they consider the questions of culture, society, and interaction with humanity. When a world and a people and a history have been built methodically, then story ideas suggest themselves.

World-building is not for everyone. It is a fairly rigorous and demanding technique, calling for more scientific training than most modern SF writers possess. Its adherents say it is fun; this is probably true only for them, and those of similar inclination. Although world-building can be valid and effective, creating vivid backgrounds and realistic, well-considered aliens when used correctly, on the whole I do not think the method should be recommended. It has dangers as well as advantages, particularly for the beginner.

A look at the work of Hal Clement, one of the most practiced of the world-builders, points up some of those dangers. Clement is precise and methodical and knows what he is about; his worlds have no seams, no mistakes. Each is unique, carefully shaped, very real. These worlds have won Clement his reputation. Unfortunately, his stories do not always match the worlds they are set on, and although Clement is often cited as being particularly good with aliens, actually the reverse is sometimes true.

Mission of Gravity, Clement's best-known novel, is a case in point. A near-classic, the story takes place on Mesklin, a disc-shaped planet with seas of liquid methane and terrible gravity. Because of the planet's shape and rotation, that gravity varies enormously — much heavier at the poles, lightest at the equator.

The protagonists of the novel are Mesklinites, aliens admirably tailored to meet the physical conditions of their world in the best world-builder fashion. They are pseudocentipedes (short-changed, since they have only 36 legs) 15 inches long, built close to the ground in deference to the immense gravitational pull. All this is fine. The Mesklinites have one big psychological quirk as well: fear of falling, since falls on Mesklin are always fatal.

Other than that, captain Barlennan of the good ship *Bree* and his crew are virtually human. Barlennan is a seafarin' man, his "alien" culture is Merry Old England or maybe colonial New England, and Barlennan himself is a sharp, salty Yankee trader. The seas of Mesklin are methane, the Mesklinites are only 15 inches long, and they have 36 legs, and all this is meaningless, because Clement fails in the last test — he has not bothered to create an *alien*. The world overshadows its inhabitants.

Star Light, a 1971 sequel to *Mission of Gravity,* is additional testimony to how world-building might go wrong. In this story Clement takes Barlennan and crew off Mesklin, to Dhrawn, another high gravity world. The passage of 17 years between the two books does not make the Mesklinites any less human or more alien; Barlennan is still Ol' Cap'n Centipede.

Both of these failings, I think, are failings of the world-builders' technique, and an all-too-common consequence of trying to write a story back-to-front. For most writers, the characters and the story come first, and that is as it should be. The world-builders are like artists who spend years designing frames, and then hurriedly paint a picture to put in them. Sometimes it works. Sometimes.

But not often enough to justify the procedure.

Tailor the Alien to the Story

There is a second method of creating aliens and alien societies, one that I think has a great deal more to recommend it than world-building. It is a method less precise and more intuitive, and it proceeds in the other direction. Writers who use this method start with a germ of a story, perhaps flash on the idea of a bizarre, colorful society peopled by strange extraterrestrials of some sort. Then they work out a world and a history to fit, after the more basic requirements like psychology are already established. And story requirements come before everything.

For this method, one rule above all: form should follow function.

Your alien has a purpose in your story, a role to play, a reason to be there; his history and his appearance and his way of thinking should be shaped so that he can play that role with maximum effectiveness. Now, you want a full-fleshed character, one who lives and breathes (even if methane) and seems real; and when you create such a monster, your creation will soon grow beyond the story-function you laid out for him. Nonetheless, the story-function comes first, and should always be kept in mind; if your alien seems to be headed in a direction that will weaken his ability to do whatever you need him to do, then you have to change that direction.

Once the bones are connected, the skeletal diagram being determined by requirements of plot, characterization and theme, then you must make your alien real. Here is where the fine hand becomes all-important, for often the small touches make or break an alien — the secondary characteristics that support the primary ones, the clever afterthoughts, the fine brushstroke and the vital little details. Do it lightly; put in bits of history and folklore from the mass you have worked out, glimpses of art and architecture casually seen, insights into language and religion and myth. Don't lecture. Mention. And make it all real.

Let's say you want to write a story about freedom and repression. You have statements you want to make, a theme, a plot, some characters. You want to show a conflict between a repressive society and an anarchist one, between order and freedom; you want to consider the moral consequences of their struggle. Fine. Only a million or so writers have done this story before, a mere thousand or two in SF, so it's still fresh and worth doing if you handle it well. Certain themes are timeless.

You decide to use aliens in your story. You can do this in any of a number of ways. Regimented aliens versus free humanity. Regimented humanity versus free aliens. Regimented aliens versus free aliens. And so on. Now, what sort of aliens should you create if you choose the first alternative? Well, you want a regimented society, an iron and repressive culture. Perhaps you want a hive mind, where individuals are nothing but nulls in the greater whole that is the society. That sort of alien has been done a good many times before, of course, but every writer brings his own eyes to a subject, so maybe you can find something fresh to make the symbol live again.

What if you choose the second alternative? Well, flight has been a symbol of freedom since the days of Icarus, so perhaps you want a race of winged aliens. Again, SF has seen a lot of winged aliens, some better than others. Writers keep doing them because the idea *is* powerful, and I suspect writers will keep on doing them for a good long time.

Let's say you decide you want to go with your winglings, put them into conflict (when I say conflict, by the way, I'm talking about dramatic conflict, not war) with humanity. That's fine. Now you have to sit down and develop a world and a history for them and this is where the rigorous techniques of the world-builders can come into good use — in building up the iceberg of information on which your aliens stand. You start with the one thing you know about them — they are flyers, symbols of freedom. A lot follows logically from there. Their world, for example, must be relatively low gravity. After all, they have to have fairly large brains for intelligence, and that in turn dictates fairly large bodies, and for a large animal to take to the air — well, low gravity is one answer. Reinforce it with other detail. They have hollow bones, like birds, say, and that means their bones probably break quite easily. Fragile fellows, these winglings.

What else do you know about them? Well, their world is low gravity, remember, so it is either a small planet or a large one with a relatively small mass, which could mean that it's metal-poor. That in turn would mean the winglings could not easily develop an Earthlike technology; you can't have an iron age without iron. So maybe they're primitives. You don't *want* them to be primitive? Oh. A small planet then, instead of a large rocky one. Don't make it too small, however, or you'll have to explain why it still has so much atmosphere. Your winglings need relatively thick air to fly in, after all.

On to social structure − borrow from birds again; group them in great flocks, make them a migratory civilization. Wait. Did you buy that? You shouldn't have. Civilizations like that have been done (Poul Anderson depicted one brilliantly in *The Man Who Counts,* later republished under the regrettable title *War of the Wing Men*), but *you* have to keep *your* story in mind. Your winged aliens were a symbol of freedom, remember? So you don't want flocks. No matter how tempting the detail, if it cripples the alien's ability to accomplish its story function, it's no good.

I could go on. The process has only begun, and a thousand decisions remain to be made. How do these aliens fly? Are they gliders, or true birds that climb under their own musclepower? What sort of history do they have? What sort of song and language? How did they evolve (there is probably an evolutionary reason *why* they are flyers, and I'd bet the ecology of their homeworld has more winged species than our own)? Religion? Myth? Eating habits? Mating habits?

Many of these decisions will work themselves out. Others will not, options will present themselves, and choices will be there waiting to be made. The way you make them will determine exactly how real and memorable your aliens are to your readers.

My motives in discussing winged aliens in particular were somewhat sneaky; for some reason, this subspecies of sentients seems to have more fascination for SF writers than virtually any others. Recently, Vonda McIntyre has won a reputation with stories of one winged race, stories like (appropriately enough) "Wings," a Nebula finalist. But she was far from the first. Wallace West wrote of winged Martians in a little-known novel called *The Bird of Time,* and Algis Budrys contributed aliens of his own in *The Amsirs and the Iron Thorn,* and none of these is the least bit like the others, or even very much like the winglings that we sketched so broadly a few paragraphs ago. Even within a narrow perimeter like "wings," there is plenty of room. For critics and readers, the comparisons can be endlessly engrossing. See how different West's flyers are from Budrys's Amsirs (because they were created for different functions, of course, everything following from there). And how utterly strange other winged aliens — say, H.P. Lovecraft's dark rubbery-winged night gaunts — are to all of them, in everything that matters except the almost incidental fact of wings.

Poul Anderson is probably the winged alien champion of the world, since he is the only author known to have turned the trick twice with complete success. First with the splendid Diomedians of *War of the Wing Men,* bat-winged and furred, and more recently in a series of novels and stories about the feathered, very avian Ythrians. *The People of the Wind,* perhaps the finest segment of the Ythri cycle, is especially worthy of note. A Hugo nominee in its year of publication, the novel explores the culture and psychology of the Ythrian colonists on Avalon, a melting-pot world they share with humanity. Although the plot revolves around a rather routine interstellar war, the background details of cross-cultural interaction are fascinating. Everything about the Ythrians hangs together, and reinforces everything else; history and religion and sexual customs, everything feels right, up to and including the shrill, trilling names. Anderson neglects nothing, and the Ythrians live. For a beginner interested in aliens, both Anderson novels should be required reading.

Anderson's work in general is of interest, actually, since

Poul is one of the best alien-assemblers in the business. He sometimes falls into the traps of world-building, and emerges with backgrounds and civilizations that are stronger than his plots and characters, but he never fails to tell a story, and unlike Clement he has never tried to pass off a New England sailing man as an alien. Generally his extraterrestrials range from the merely adequate to the excellent.

Larry Niven is another prominent modern author of the hard science school whose works should be studied, since he too has created some interesting aliens, notably the kzinti and the Pierson's puppeteers. Despite his virtues, however, Niven's solidly-built creations have much less depth than Anderson's, thanks to a dire lack of the supporting detail that Anderson does so well. The typical Niven alien tends to overdone simplicity, with one trait becoming all (the puppeteers are embodied cowardice and intellect, the kzin are carnivore aggression), the key to everything the creature says and does. Of course, real aliens may very well be like that. But people aren't, and neither are Anderson's complex aliens, weighed down with their burdens of myth and culture and social restraint.

Aliens of Mystery

Although Niven and Clement and Anderson are very different writers in several ways, they nonetheless have much in common, and all of them represent what might be seen as one "school" of alienology. Some of these writers succeed better than others, but each of them is trying to do approximately the same thing.

Aliens are bigger than any school built to contain them, however, and the brightly-lit, tightly-extrapolated and well-understood humanoids of Anderson and Niven occupy only a few small corners in the galaxy of science fiction. There is room for other sorts of aliens as well, creatures less of the intellect and more of the emotions, beings of mystery as well as history. On paper, the most visible difference is a simple shift of emphasis — less is explained, and the subjects spoken of relate more to the soft sciences than to the hard. The mood of these aliens is very unlike that of the Ythrians, but the models are no less valid and interesting.

Consider the alien races of Jack Vance, for example: all color and dash and intricate custom. Or some of Robert Heinlein's lovely creations: the invaders in *The Puppet Masters,* the Mother Thing and her civilization from *Have Space Suit, Will Travel.* Or the work of some talented younger writers: the moody, myth-drenched Cian that Gardner Dozois gave us in his brilliant novella, "Strangers," or Michael Bishop's mysterious Asadi. My own aliens — The Shkeen in "A Song for Lya," the Jaenshi from "And Seven Times Never Kill Man," the numerous crossworlds races in "The Stone City" — tend to have more in common with Vance and Dozois than with Anderson or Niven, although I would like to think they are primarily my own, and different from anything that has gone before.

Aliens of this type often seem more *alien* than others, stranger, not quite so easy to explain or understand or communicate with. This does not mean that they are not as well worked out; it is a shift in authorial intent, not in authorial skill. Generally, it means the writer is telling us less (although even this is not always true — few authors tell us nearly as much as Vance), and more importantly he is telling us different things; it means that the author is telling a horror story or a romance or a fable, rather than one of Poul Anderson's tales of war and political intrigue. These aliens live on darker, wilder worlds than Avalon or Ythri, and drink more heavily of the wine of mystery. They are closer, perhaps, to the primal alien, to the ghosts and demons of the old fantasists. But none of this makes them the lazy man's aliens; the same sort of work still must be done to make them effective, even as figures of fear and wonder. The old fantasists, remember, knew all about their ghosts.

The Colour Out of Space Is Never Out of Mind

It is possible that when man does go at last to the stars, the other intelligences that he will meet will be like nothing remotely humanoid. Possibly humanity will not even recognize them as intelligences, they will be so far removed from us and our concerns. Or — even if they are recognized — communication and mutual understanding, even on the most basic levels, may well be impossible.

Very few SF writers have ever attempted to depict beings of a truly alien nature in their stories. The job is understandably difficult — to make the reader grasp something that is perhaps bigger than humanity, or so different as to be forever beyond reach. Fred Hoyle tried (and failed, I think) in a novel called *The Black Cloud.* Other writers have tried, and fallen even farther from the mark.

The two who come closest are an odd pair; Stanislaw Lem and H.P. Lovecraft.

In *Solaris,* Lem created a marvelous sentient ocean, a being of such power and mystery and strangeness that it is virtually impossible to forget. The alien ocean Solaris *made* Lem's book, an otherwise slow and difficult read, and assures the novel continued life.

In much the same way, the stories of H.P. Lovecraft will live because of their eldritch aliens. Shadow-shapes of fevered intensity, they transcend Lovecraft's sometimes broken-backed style and fondness for words like "eldritch," his total lack of characterization, his deaf ear for dialogue. Lovecraft had all of the flaws that it is possible for a writer to have, but his works survive because he understood the Alien. Better than Lem, better than anyone, he touched the very essence of strangeness (although his admirers and imitators took his fine creations after his death and turned them into fourth-rate aliens indeed).

Yet, even with Lovecraft, the iceberg is there, floating lower in the water so that less is readily apparent, but still there. Those who might object that Lovecraft's creations were not science fictional, or were not worked out with any care or detail — those are people who probably have not read *The Shadow Out of Time,* or *At the Mountains of Madness,* or — his finest and most totally alien myth-child — *The Colour Out of Space.*

The color is an alien being, something from beyond our world, like no Earthly shade, more outré even than Lem's ocean. In one of the memorable scenes of the story, the protagonist sees it dancing and straining brightly on the farmhouse and field and trees before launching itself back up into the night. But when the brightness has made its ascent, and the tortured landscape is dark again, he sees that a small bit of the color remains, having risen briefly only to fall again, and linger at the bottom of the well.

The passage is written in Lovecraft's thick adjective-heavy prose, but it has power for all that. It is a moment that will be remembered.

As Solaris will be remembered, Solaris with its strange formations, rolling beneath twin suns.

And the Martians of H.G. Wells, intellects vast and cool and unsympathetic, riding their war machines.

And Heinlein's terrible puppet masters, slugs that rode a man's back and enslaved his mind and soul. And the flock of bat-winged Lannachska, bringing war to the rafts of the Drak'honai. And Rama, the great alien spaceship. And Tschai with all its peoples.

And ... and ... and ....

For all the headaches and the worries and the problems, yes, yes, aliens are still worth doing.

The final article in this volume is, in many ways, the most valuable. Writing is, for some, merely a hobby, while for others it is the way to make a living. In both instances, however, there is a common denominator: money. How to spend it and how to save it. For writing, as perhaps for few other professions, tax and supply savings are a major consideration, and there is no one more qualified to advise you on the ins and outs of such mysterious ways as the current Treasurer of SFWA, **andrew j offutt.**

Besides his labor on behalf of SFWA, andrew offutt has been a successful insurance executive, and is now a fulltime writer under several pseudonyms with well over three dozen SF and non-SF books to his credit; he has been Toastmaster and Guest of Honor at many conventions, has a houseful of offuttspring and a wife, Jodie, who is a fine author in her own right.

CHAPTER 10:

Money Is Valuable: Save It!

by
andrew j offutt

Agents, publishers, book distributors, jobbers and book-dealers are business people. Creators, artists, are not "supposed to be." There do exist sound reasons for the difference in personalities and for the nonbusinesslike mental set of artists — but there's no reason we can't do our best to operate as businesspersons.

Other sections of this book tell you, one hopes, how to plot, to research, to study, to stay abreast, to "think SF" or to extrapolate, and probably how to build a planet — on paper. To do all this you must spend money, from the first book or journal you buy for research to the postage on the manuscript. Every time you find an editor perceptive enough to agree with you that yours is a good story, you will make — or at least receive — some money.

Let's talk about how to save money, then, and how to keep all you can of what you receive for the product of your mind. It should be said early that I am a personal sort of person, and that this will be a personal sort of article, with a high "I" count — even for a writer. I am not a tax expert or an accountant or a fed. I'm a writer; my writing is the sole and soul support of me, my family and our dentists. I do my very best to run me *as a business.*

People who aren't making much have more *need* to save money. Yet those who have "more than they need" (whatever that is; coffee, liquor and postage keep going up!) can afford less economizing . . . but seldom operate that way. They often know more and/or have accountants, and thus may spend even less in the conduct of their business, *and* deduct more at tax time. (The economizing practices of large corporations, as I learned in my years as a salesman for a multinational company and then in the insurance business as both salesman and executive, are incredible. Also chintzy, appalling, and — effective.)

To begin with, *get receipts.* It's plain dumb to pick up a 98c or even a 49c pen at the drugstore for cash: that thing's deductible and you might well need another dollar or so in deductions, come the Ides of April. Buy everything you can-by charge or check. It is all deductible: correction tape, cartridges for felt- or ballpens, typewriter ribbons, postage, every scrap of paper, the 49c yellow highlighter you use to make research easier — all of it.

It Takes Lots of Paper

An expensive way to buy bond is in tablets at drugstores and campus bookstores; even buying it a hundred sheets at a time is silly, because it costs more that way. So is using fancy "look-at-me" paper. Though you must lay out more originally for 500 or more sheet quantities, you do save money that way. Nice heavy, fancy, crisp bond looks prettier. But *because* it's crisp, it tends to crease and bend and *stay* that way, rather than curl or rumple in the manner of lighter paper. It also costs more both to buy and to mail. For those several reasons, I used 16-pound bond for 15 years. No watermarks, no fancy finish; editors are not going to buy a story because the *paper* dazzles them. They do *not* care, so long as the paper is white and relatively unmessy (most like to see some corrections; it assures them you Care).

Now the scamps seem to have stopped making 16-pound bond (the lightest that is usable) for submission. I've had to go to the *next* lightest, 20-pound ... and up have gone my postage costs for mss of the same length. Both 16 and 20 look fine. A batch is less bulky than heavier stuff with or without watermark or grain, and thus weighs less, and thus requires less postage. *My* 60,000-worder may be a quarter-inch thinner than yours if you use expensive bond (and thinner still if you do silly wasteful things such as leaving two-inch margins all around). Too, if you use 10-pitch Pica and I use 12-pitch Elite type, the difference in words-per-page (I get 330) and thus ms height — and thus weight — may be a half-inch or more. Try measuring off a half-inch of paper and putting it on the postal scales! If New York is, say, Zone 4 for you as it is for me, you may spend from 22c (doubled for return postage) to 66c — *doubled* — more than I would, every time you send a novel to Manhattan (or, *sigh,* the same novel).

That means I have more beer-money than you ....

You can save a lot more by using boxes for *storage only,* and eschewing use of those mailing envelopes stuffed with shredded paper. The ones with the plastic bubbles inside protect the ms — and are *light.*

This writer has his bond cut for him, locally. Thus I pay nothing for advertising, packaging, jobber, salesman's commission, and retailer. "My" printer drags out a ream of 16- or 20-pound, cuts it into 8½ x 11 sheets (21.6cm x 27.9), and wraps it in brown paper. (Gosh mom, personal business!)

A ream yields 2,000 sheets, for which he still charges me less than ten bucks. With sales tax, two plastic-wrapped batches of 50 sheets each cost over a dollar at the store. Multiply that by 20 to price 2,000 sheets — and note that *my second thousand sheets are "free"!* (And don't let your offspring in a typing class pay that silly 49c for 50 sheets!)

Check with a printer. For ten minutes' work he can sell you a ream and make cost plus ten. Twenty pound bond (16 if you can find it) takes type well from any machine. It also takes correction type, which I prefer to that time-consuming liquid gop. Again: no editor has ever said a word about my paper or my grayish corrections, even those who've bought, literally, dozens of mss from me.

First Drafts and Second Sheets

My first draft envelopes, correspondence files and carbon copies stay skinny because I use the cheapest and thinnest paper for first machine drafts and all carbon copies. Sure, there's onionskin. There is also that less expensive, thinner stuff that's slick on one side and "rough" on the other. A box of a thousand sheets with COPY printed on one side is more than a box of plain (about 30c more), and a thousand sheets *unboxed* is a quarter less than *that.* (Prices, of course, are subject to change without any notice from me.) Why should you be paying people for *boxes;* you can beg those from the nearest university, bank, or big or little business office — or get them out of their garbage cans.

Ask the office supply store or campus bookstore to order it for you in packages, not boxes, and without COPY on it. So it's a little trouble — you're buying, they're selling, and they're making money. Let them know you are one of those magic creatures, a W*R*I*T*E*R. And, in this sort of case, if they ask if you've published and you haven't — LIE!

The last time I bought this stuff, I ordered a case; ten packages: 10,000 sheets. That way the cost came down to four sheets for a penny. (Onion is about two-a-penny, in thousand-sheet lots.)

By the way, when you're using this skinny paper for first machine drafts, pad it with a sheet of something else — a piece from all that junkmail you get, for instance. You can use it over and over — and make your machine's platen last longer. They cost money too, you know.

I *know* some of you use that tan or yaller stuff called newspaper. Maybe you get it free. But lord all Friday, it's so *bulky!* Correspondence files fill up in months; novel carbons have to be kept in *boxes,* and I suppose intermediate drafts would have to be stored in detergent cases.

Years ago I bought a hand model three-hole punch (and deducted its cost). Now and again I buy another half-dozen of those cardboard folders with the three staples mounted in the center. They cost *about* 20c at drugstores and campus bookstores. So: having used skinny paper for the carbon copy of my ms, I punch that hunk of posterity with three holes, secure it in the folder, mark the novel's name on the edge of the folder, and stack 'em on a shelf. Carbons of a hundred novels do take a lot of shelf-space — but much less than if they were on heavier paper and had to go in boxes. (Carbons of shorter mss can be stored in manila envelopes. Don't *buy* them; recycle those you receive in the mail. They needn't be sealed.)

Paper, folders, three-hole punch, and labels are all deductible. Get a receipt, pay by check and *keep records.*

Any drugstore or discount store I've ever visited had stacks of packages of lined ring-binder paper: 500 sheets for less than a dollar. It is perfect for handwritten drafts and notetaking — when I run out of what I usually use: the backs of the children's school papers! You can pay a lot more for the same paper, elsewhere or in smaller quantities. Using feltpoint pen and rubber fingertips (those nipple-looking things bankers use to count money) saves my fingers — or helps preserve them, anyhow. All deductible.

From Cheapskate to Ecological Hero

If you're *looking* for deductions, the plastic carbon sheets that are guaranteed reusable a hundred times are convenient — and can be used 60 or so times. Otherwise — I haven't bought any carbon paper for years and years. You needn't. Thousands and thousands of sheets are being used once, all around you, and thrown away. They come out of *sets:* three- or four-sheet forms, used by insurance companies, various college departments, other businesses, banks, courthouse offices. A few blanks are filled in, the sets pulled apart for various recipients and files, and the almost-mint carbon sheets are pitched, without military honors.

Go get 'em. I recommend you ask your own insurance agent first. Go to the office. *Ask.* (Insurance is a very competitive business, and they are *nice.*) Mine even began saving them for me, in big manila envelopes. As an interesting sidelight: someone in that office, realizing what a sharpie I was, began using those barely-"used" carbons in the office — and now they don't buy carbon paper, either. (They still save some for me. I, after all, was their "efficiency expert," by accident.)

If an office uses a computer system, the Iron Brain spits out a mile-long set of printed sheets, perforated, with carbon between. Thirty days later it's all pitched. Ask for that, spend a few minutes tearing off the carbon sheets at the perforations, and . . . recycle. (They will usually go about four times.) Maybe you can use the backs of the print-out sheets, too, for first drafts or letters. (You get more use from carbon by rolling the paper into the typewriter before inserting carbon. That way you vary the interval, and use the carbon "between the lines.")

Yes, I also turn out the lights when I leave a room. Once I was just a cheapskate . . . . Now I am a planetwide recycling ecological hero!

That's about it on paper. Trivial? OK; it's your money. I began inventing all these money-saving methods because I was pore, and because I grew up thinking that conspicuous consumption is obscene. You too can save money and be a hero; pick your own reason.

Postage And Stuff

A lot of money is dribbled away and undeducted, on postage – and yet getting a receipt every time you mail off a ms is a drag.

In 1968 I bought a small postage scale for four dollars – and deducted its cost, as it was bought solely for the purpose of weighing mss. The scale is now well out of date because of postal rate increases. OK; it says one ounce is 06 and five ounces are 30; I can multiply. I can also write checks, so I buy postage in quantity, by check – and get from the PO people those little folders that give rates and postal zones. Best is to make up a "grocery list" in advance: amount of postage to be purchased, perhaps dependent upon how short you are that month .... Say you want to stock in ten three's, ten 30s, and six 50-centers (with mean-lookin Lucy Stone), plus 20 eights (for postcards; make your own!), and a sheet of 50 tens (ask for commemoratives and decorate your envelopes).

Print that out and tote it up: about $12. If that's too mean a chunk of money this month, buy half as many tens or skip the 50s. Just skip the little folders of stamps they so love to sell you, too: those and stamp machines are legal robbery.

Sending a "normal" novel to Manhattan used to cost me two 50s, two 20s and a three. That was first class for under two pounds – a lot more from California! It's more now, of course. (No, I do *not* use Special Fourth Class Rate. I want to be sure it *gets* there, and *this* year, so I pay the U.S.P. "S" its protection money. You can get a sheet of First Class stickers, too – and my gosh, they are *free*!)

Incidentally, it's nice to know agent or editor received your ms. Simple: I enclose an unlined filecard, addressed to myself and bearing an 8c stamp, typed as follows:

andy: Received your story _____.
                                              date

Other comment: _____.

Agent or editor fills it in and sticks it in the Out basket. If you don't receive it within ten days after mailing the ms — assuming you sent First Class — it's time to start checking.

With scales and stamps on hand, you deduct every cent of your business postage. Too, you can stamp your mss before going to the post office, saving time and trouble for you and the clerks there. (Let them know you've done it, and be sure you're right: they'll love you.) Neither you nor they have to bother with those dummy little receipts; a check made out to "Postmaster" *is* a receipt. If you just love the USP "S" and the IR "S," merely pay for the letter to Aunt Matilda by not-deducting a couple of bucks' worth of your postage on your Schedule C.

Fingers and Ribands

If you handwrite first drafts and/or are a two- or three-finger typist as I am, time will come when your fingers will splay and get sore very quickly. Be warned: avoid corrugated pens and pencils with those squared-off striations down the barrel. They're put there to keep schoolchildren's pencils from rolling off their desks, and over the long haul, they will wipe out your fingers. That is why I use feltpens: one doesn't have to lean on 'em. And that is why I protect my splayed fingers (and thumb too, when handwriting) with those rubber fingertips I've already mentioned. I recommend them to your attention; my fingers had been sore for a couple of years *before* I thought of them, and one purpose of this book is to *share;* to let you profit by our knowledge — and from our mistakes.

There is an ugly corollary between patience and ecological concern — and affluence. Maybe you're flush and "don't have to" do this, but ... typewriter ribbons can be made to last longer by being *oiled.*

You simply take the ribbon off, before it begins striking letters the color of the cuff of a ten-year-old blouse. Nestle it in a cupping piece of (used!) aluminum foil big enough to wrap it a couple of times. Dribble a very few drops of normal machine oil on the ribbon. Snug it. Stash it somewhere, roll a new ribbon into the machine, and go back to work.

After a month or so, unwrap the oiled ribbon and *let it lie there for a day or so.* Then roll it into the machine, and use it. No, not on submission drafts; that's a small portion of the total job anyhow. Oiled, that ribbon you'd have thrown away (or inflicted on your friends via gray correspondence) becomes a "new" one for first drafts and correspondence. Voilà: something like one and three-fourths ribbons for the price of one.

There's another way of saving money on ribbons. Like most ways of saving money, it takes a little capital outlay. The man who services my typewriter — let's not mention any names but the three initials begin with my favorite letter: I — says the ribbons his company makes for my machine, though I consider them expensive, will last twice as long as others and thus aren't expensive at all. Maybe so; I disagree. This is an article of opinion by a fiercely independent and opinionated person (which is to say, a writer).

For several years, I have been buying my ribbons by mail. I suppose I shouldn't say from where/whom, but the guy has been advertising in *Writer's Digest* ever since I can remember. He sells my ribbons, by the dozen, for about half what they cost in stores or from the typewriter manufacturer. Prices vary depending on the machine you use. When I order a dozen, I send my check: it becomes my receipt. Since the old red-black ribbon is still made, and so are gray ones (!

Sort of like pre-faded jeans, I suppose), I carefully specify "jet-black all-black, nylon."

In the past four years, I have ordered nine dozen ribbons from that man I have never met but think of as a friend. What other friend has saved me some $80 in four years?

If you think all this is elementary, pontificatory, or just plain silly-unnecessary: OK; go write a book.

For those of you who are saying Thanks because you've learned something and know you'll be thankful after saving a bit of money: you go write a book, too!

And now we come down to *It*.

Beware the Ides of April

The time to start preparing to treat yourself fairly next April 15 ... is April 16! You remember you're in business; you charge or pay by check and/or obtain receipts, you set up a place to keep them, and you make special notes in the checkbook.

Bear in mind that the idea is to get all you can off Schedule C, Profit or Loss from Business or Profession, *before* you arrive at the adjusted gross income figure on form 1040 (a number that lives in infamy transcended only by 12/7/1941 — though the latter is more easily understood).

Total income goes at the top of Schedule C, and every last possible expense in your professional pursuit should come off below. To be thorough and provide backup, you will need to include a separate sheet or sheets, labeled "EXPLANA-TION: Schedule C" or something similarly brilliantly original. Make sure you cut two carbons: for the state, and for your files. Keep it right there with your copy of the return.

Getting totally reasoned and reasonable answers from Internal Revenue is about as easy as obtaining a reasoned, reasonable, legal and absolute definition of pornography. Both are subject to interpretation, meaning the whim of an individual — and to appeal. A few years ago I was subjected to a massive audit. The demands and threats, all on printed forms, were manifestly unreasonable. The faceless form-sender avowed that I owed another $400 (an absolutely *enormous* sum, then), and that I had to come to them with every receipt — separated and annotated. (They even sent back, denied, the notarized affidavit from my landlord — I had a downtown office then — showing the amount I had paid him in rent!)

It was scary, Tough Duty, and fighting in the dark. Also fruitless — until I quit messing with the hired help and spent all one Sunday writing — four drafts; good copy! — a letter to the Boss: the President. Results were nigh-instantaneous. A letter from the Undersecretary of the Treasury. A letter from the District Director in a city many miles away. And a visit from a GS-13. We talked. He examined my records and receipts. (Look, I had *earned* less than twenty thousand that year; I was a small patootie, and some clerk's idiocy cost, doubtless, my entire taxes for that year!) His decision: he was mad at his people; they were wrong. I was right. I owed no additional taxes.

Nevertheless, it's necessary to repeat the disclaimer. I am not a tax expert, or an accountant, or a fed, and I am merely going to tell you what *I* do. It is certainly possible that I will be checked again. (Hey, in fairness to the unfair, let me add that a couple of years ago "they" sent me back a note; their machine had caught me in a simple mathematical error, and ... *I had overpaid!*)

You can believe that I keep records. I am prepared to prove that I subscribed to the magazine *British History Illustrated* because I was working on a series about Richard the Lion-Hearted and another set in "Dark Age" Erin ... and I am prepared to prove that I did indeed buy a $1.49 automatic pencil for use in my profession. Your canceled check for this book is valuable: it proves you bought it. And certainly you bought it as a professional aid!

A simple list of deductible items will wind up this article. Between now and then, let's talk about deductible and probably-deductible not-so-simple items.

But My Trip to Acapulco Was for Research . . . .

If it feels like a professional journal or a book of aid, it probably is. Hence a subscription to any of the writers' magazines, the purchase of an annual Markets book, the purchase of this book, even a not-quite-professional journal to which you may subscribe for market and other information in the field — all are deductible.

Part of the business of a writer is to study and seek to understand humankind: what's gone on and what's going on. Yet I have never attempted to deduct my subscriptions to *Newsweek, Psychology Today* or *National Geographic,* though I use a yellow highlighter (all right, Hi-Liter) in each issue of each, and make notes therefrom. Maybe I am being too cautious.

Because I was writing about the Third Crusade, though, I was sure of myself in deducting Zoë Oldenbourg's *The Crusades,* among others, and the expensive *Larousse Encyclopedia of Ancient and Medieval History.* When others, those for whom Book-of-the-Month *et al* exist, were reading *Handbook of PSI Discoveries* and *Secret Life of Plants* and making "Oooh!" and "Aah!" noises, I bought them too . . . and wrote a long novelet, a "biotronic" (and thus SF) murder mystery. And I deducted cost of both these books, too. *I bought them for research,* you see.

I have read that a writer can take off a lot more subscriptions and books — I did deduct a 24-volume witchcraft/magic encyclopedia — but I am ever cautious, and deduct only those to which I can specifically point as having provided beneficial aid to research. It seems smart to think about each expenditure, and to behave yourself as though an IR man were going to drop by tomorrow and ask you to prove your expenses.

A journalist or a stringer can deduct the cost of trips to get an interview or a story, *unless he is on full expense account.* So can you, provided you make the trip in order to further your writing career, and sell something now and again. My trip to the Apollo 14 shot should probably have been deductible because I was and am a creator of SF. As it was, I wrote one article and did one radio program about it, which made it very specifically *research.*

Like most other groups, the Science Fiction Writers of America annually votes and makes awards for excellence in novel, short story, etc. Awards are made at a dinner in Manhattan or on the West Coast, in conjunction with a little "convention" of a couple or three days' duration. There is programming, with panels and lectures. Editors and publishers come, and one can and does discuss specific projects with them; deals have been done at bars and over coffee far more than once. Hence a trip to such a get-together is deductible for all of us. Keep records, including notes as to whom you talked with about what business matter. You'll find the amount allowed by IR for mileage surprisingly good — particularly if all you've been acccustomed to is the pittance that "normal people" are allowed to deduct for trips in conjunction with the maintenance or improvement of their health . . . .

Make notes on meals, tips, cab fare, and *keep them.*

The matter of taking your spouse along, and whether you can deduct his/her portion of planefare and hotel bill, is not only tricky but a bit moot, and I'm going to suggest you talk with an accountant about it. For years I did not; I was scoffed at and advised to by so many colleagues that I began deducting the whole hotel bill, rather than taking off only the single rate and thus not deducting my wife's expenses. Remember, though, that your particular situation is involved; I am a professional, fulltime writer, and my Jodie not only does the final typing of my mss, she handles assorted business matters as well — and helps keep me sane on trips.

If you are MC or Guest of Honor or Guest Speaker, you must report any payments made to you — and by the same token, you are allowed to subtract any expenses incurred; sometimes one's ego or need for change prompts one to say yes and go and show off even though the group's "gratuity" or "honorarium" (they never seem to use nasty words such as money, fee, payment) doesn't cover your time and expenses. If you *want* to go, say, to Manhattan, try to set up (in advance by letter followed by phone call) meetings with editors and agent(s). The trip thus becomes *business* and your visit to Aunt Mary and the UN Building incidental, right? Deductions!

You might go to speak to a high school class or club such as Kiwanis or Book Society or Garden Club for "love" — but love plays no part in the proceedings of 15th April; deduct the mileage and any other specific expenses. (Sorry; *not* the cleaning of your best suit.)

End trips, which if you're in government you call *junkets*. (These matters of Big Government are most difficult for us little people to understand, but I believe a "junket" is a trip to Acapulco to study the interior of hotel rooms, watering holes and nightclubs, with a view to returning with that information to aid the people of the United States.)

But Mister Fed, I DO Write in the Bathroom ....

About anyone who writes can deduct a piece of his/her apartment or home, whether leased or owned. Some recent rulings have really liberalized the interpretation of using a portion of one's home as office; in one case, incredibly, the court's ruling was more liberal than ever I'd have been! May his name be forever blessed.

If you write in your rented or owned house, apartment, room or garret, you *can* deduct a portion of the rent or housepayments. Maybe you have an accountant to call and check with, or know one; if you're in the city, you can always call IR and ask them. And if you are told NoWay, ask for that dummy's superior; he or she is *wrong.* You can. If you are not now, you're wasting money. — Begin!

In my case, I own a home with seven rooms, a kitchen and two bathrooms. There are also three big halls, but they don't count; they're not rooms, but ways to get places. One of the seven rooms is my office. All of it. I *could* have measured the whole house, *skipping the bathrooms* (don't ask *me;* maybe writers aren't supposed to, uh, do that), and then determined what percentage of the floorspace the office occupies. But since bathrooms don't count but kitchens do and the office is thus one of eight rooms, I handle it that way.

The bank and I own the house. To begin with, I deduct ⅛ of that portion of my monthly payments that is interest; the teller divides it on the payment book every month. (The balance of the interest is deductible elsewhere; right now we are working to get every possible item off *Schedule C.*) Next I total the principal payments for the year and deduct ⅛ of that — and perform the same exercise with the power and heat bills. (This operation, like that of computing amount spent on gasoline takes on all those little gasoline bills, is a horrid business. Obviously, you *need* one of those $20 calculators, since you are a businessperson and are frequently paid by the word. *Deduct the cost of the calculator.*)

The above is Law, the legal way, and certainly I'd have no trouble proving that the office is both a deduction and approximately 12.5 percent or ⅛ of the house's available rooms. A portion of the property tax bill, remember, is similarly deductible. So are the bookshelves you buy for the office portion, or the file cabinet — better depreciate that. It's easy.

The same holds if you are renting, though in that case I assume you take off room-percentage of the whole total; there is no (visible) interest. The same holds true if you are leasing a two-room apartment — or even *one* room. Some chunk of that piece of real estate is your "office." You isolate the area, figuratively speaking, and figure the percentage — with care — and deduct that percentage of rent and utilities. A starving writer (to all too many, that is redundant) in the traditional garret can, if he writes there, measure the total floorspace and then the area occupied by his "writing HQ" (desk, chair, cabinet). Do *not* try deducting half the rent and utilities if you sit on the edge of the bed with the typewriter on your knees. You won't hear the tramp of booted feet in the night — just one of those scary impersonal forms, giving you orders.

Now, in order to deduct writing expenses, you must of course show that you write as a matter of business. According to the I.R."S.," that means showing a profit at least two years in every five — or *proving through your records* that this isn't a hobby; that you are *trying* to write for profit. Otherwise, your writing *is* classified as a hobby, and you may deduct expenses only to the extent that you profit — if ever.

True, it's all too easy to put in 20 hours' work on a story and receive a penny a word. You can call that a profit only if your time is worth absolutely nothing. Even for money, I'd never admit it!

Again: I'm not a taxman. If you have questions, you'd better get with a friendly accountant or (try to) find a friendly revenooer. The Feds' publication 587, "Tax Information on Operating a Business in Your Home," and publication 17, "Your Federal Income Tax," will be of some value.

Obviously if in any given year you sell one little story (a gem, naturally; a sweetheart of a man named Clifford Simak once wrote me that there are no little stories; they're all *Good* stories), for $60, you can certainly find deductions totaling $59. Shucks, you made better than one percent profit, which puts you ahead of a lot of corporations.

Unfortunately, I know of no depletion allowances for midnight oil.

Checklist of Simple Deductible Items:

ink
pens
pen cartridge refills
pencil(s)
pencil leads, erasers
yellow marker(s)!
paper clips
file boxes
index cards
ring binders
journals
professional dues (e.g.: SFWA)
long-distance calls
rubber fingertips
typewriter (depreciation schedule)
typewriter ribbon
typewriter parts, repairs
typewriter: lease agreement on
typewriter: service agreement on
PAPER: lined, bond, second sheets: ALL
erasers
postage
stamp pad
stamp pad *ink!*
name/address stamp(s)
envelopes
file folders
file cabinet(s) (depreciate)
paid typist(s)
notebooks, all sizes
research books, journals
mileage (specific projects)
portion of phone bill

... and any little thing the above list may remind you of. And I am sorry. The three absolute necessities of a writer's trade and craft are, to my knowledge, not deductible. So save what you can otherwise: buy your coffee, cigarettes and booze by the case. And — write on!

Special thanks to Don Burg, city manager of H&R Block in Cincinnati, and to Joyzell M. Friason, public affairs officer of the Internal Revenue Service in Cincinnati, for their advice for the taxes portion of this article.

THE NEBULA AWARD WINNERS

1965: BEST NOVEL . . . . DUNE . . . . by Frank Herbert
BEST NOVELLA . . . . THE SALIVA TREE . . . . Brian Aldiss
HE WHO SHAPES . . . . Roger Zelazny
BEST NOVELET . . . . THE DOORS OF HIS FACE,
THE LAMPS OF HIS MOUTH . . . . Roger Zelazny
BEST SHORT STORY . . . . REPENT, HARLEQUIN, SAID
THE TICKTOCK MAN . . . . Harlan Ellison

1966: BEST NOVEL . . . . FLOWERS FOR ALGERNON . . . . . . Daniel Keyes
BABEL-17 . . . . Samuel R. Delany
BEST NOVELLA . . . . THE LAST CASTLE . . . . Jack Vance
BEST NOVELET . . . . CALL HIM LORD . . . . Gordon R. Dickson
BEST SHORT STORY . . . . THE SECRET PLACE . . . . Richard McKenna

1967: BEST NOVEL . . . . THE EINSTEIN INTERSECTION . . . Samuel R. Delany
BEST NOVELLA . . . . BEHOLD THE MAN . . . . Michael Moorcock
BEST NOVELET . . . . GONNA ROLL THE BONES . . . . . . Fritz Leiber
BEST SHORT STORY . . . . AYE, AND GOMORRAH . . . . Samuel R. Delany

1968: BEST NOVEL . . . . RITE OF PASSAGE . . . . Alexei Panshin
BEST NOVELLA . . . . DRAGONRIDER . . . . Anne McCaffrey
BEST NOVELET . . . . MOTHER TO THE WORLD . . . . . . Richard Wilson
BEST SHORT STORY . . . . THE PLANNERS . . . . Kate Wilhelm

1969: BEST NOVEL . . . . THE LEFT HAND OF DARKNESS . . Ursula K. Le Guin
BEST NOVELLA . . . . A BOY AND HIS DOG . . . . Harlan Ellison
BEST NOVELET . . . . TIME CONSIDERED AS A HELIX
OF SEMI-PRECIOUS STONES . . . . Samuel R. Delany
BEST SHORT STORY . . . . PASSENGERS . . . . Robert Silverberg

1970: BEST NOVEL . . . . RINGWORLD . . . . Larry Niven
BEST NOVELLA . . . . ILL MET IN LANKHMAR . . . . Fritz Leiber
BEST NOVELET . . . . SLOW SCULPTURE . . . . Theodore Sturgeon
BEST SHORT STORY . . . . (no award) . . . .

1971: BEST NOVEL . . . . A TIME OF CHANGES . . . . Robert Silverberg
BEST NOVELLA . . . . THE MISSING MAN . . . . Katherine MacLean
BEST NOVELET . . . . THE QUEEN OF AIR AND
DARKNESS . . . . Poul Anderson
BEST SHORT STORY . . . . GOOD NEWS FROM THE
VATICAN . . . . Robert Silverberg

1972: BEST NOVEL . . . . THE GODS THEMSELVES . . . . Isaac Asimov
BEST NOVELLA . . . . A MEETING WITH MEDUSA . . . . . Arthur C. Clarke
BEST NOVELET . . . . GOAT SONG . . . . Poul Anderson
BEST SHORT STORY . . . . WHEN IT CHANGED . . . . Joanna Russ

1973: BEST NOVEL . . . . RENDEZVOUS WITH RAMA . . . . . Arthur C. Clarke
BEST NOVELLA . . . . THE DEATH OF DOCTOR ISLAND . Gene Wolfe

```
BEST NOVELET . . . . . . . . . . OF MIST, AND GRASS,
                                 AND SAND . . . . . . . . . . . . . . . Vonda McIntyre
BEST SHORT STORY . . . . . . . LOVE IS THE PLAN, THE PLAN
                                 IS DEATH . . . . . . . . . . . . . . . . James Tiptree, Jr.
DRAMATIC PRESENTATION . . SOYLENT GREEN.
```

1974: BEST NOVEL . . . . THE DISPOSSESSED . . . . Ursula K. Le Guin
BEST NOVELLA . . . . BORN WITH THE DEAD . . . . Robert Silverberg
BEST NOVELET . . . . IF THE STARS ARE GODS . . . . . . Gordon Eklund &
                                                                     Gregory Benford
BEST SHORT STORY . . . . THE DAY BEFORE THE
                                 REVOLUTION . . . . Ursula K. Le Guin
DRAMATIC PRESENTATION . . SLEEPER.
GRAND MASTER AWARD . . . . Robert A. Heinlein

1975: BEST NOVEL . . . . THE FOREVER WAR . . . . Joe Haldeman
BEST NOVELLA . . . . HOME IS THE HANGMAN . . . . . . Roger Zelazny
BEST NOVELET . . . . SAN DIEGO LIGHTFOOT SUE . . . . Tom Reamy
BEST SHORT STORY . . . . CATCH THAT ZEPPELIN . . . . Fritz Leiber
DRAMATIC PRESENTATION . . YOUNG FRANKENSTEIN.
GRAND MASTER AWARD . . . . Jack Williamson

(Note: the year stated is the year of publication; Nebulas are awarded the following year.)

A NEW WRITER'S BIBLIOGRAPHY

This list is by no means inclusive, yet it will give the new writer an excellent sampling of the direction in which science fiction is heading, and where it has been.

Asimov, IsAac	ASIMOV'S GUIDE TO SCIENCE	Basic Books
Asimov, Isaac	THE HUGO WINNERS, I & II	Doubleday
Asimov, Isaac	THE EARLY ASIMOV	Doubleday
Bretnor, Reginald	SCIENCE FICTION, TODAY AND TOMORROW	Harper & Row
Blish, James	CITIES IN FLIGHT	Avon
Carr, Terry	THE BEST SCIENCE FICTION OF THE YEAR	Ballantine
Carr, Terry	UNIVERSE (series)	Ace, Random, Doubleday
Ferman, Edward	THE BEST FROM FANTASY AND SCIENCE FICTION (series)	Doubleday
Heinlein, Robert	THE PAST THROUGH TOMORROW	Berkley
Gunn, James	ALTERNATE WORLDS	Prentice-Hall
Knight, Damon	SCIENCE FICTION OF THE THIRTIES	Bobbs-Merrill
Merrill, Judith	ANNUAL OF THE YEAR'S BEST SCIENCE FICTION	Doubleday
Orwell, George	NINETEEN EIGHTY-FOUR	Signet
Silverberg, Robert	NEW DIMENSIONS (series)	Doubleday
Silverberg, Robert	ALPHA (series)	Ballantine
Silverberg, Robert	SCIENCE FICTION HALL OF FAME, I & II	Doubleday
Sagan, Carl	THE COSMIC CONNECTION	Doubleday
Wollheim, Don	WORLD'S BEST SF (series)	DAW

Scientific American	Locus	Fantasy & Science Fiction
Science Digest	Analog	Galaxy
Natural History	Amazing	
Psychology Today	Fantastic	

THE NEBULA AWARDS STORIES, various editors, (series) Pocket Books
Harper & Row

INDEX

Other Useful Publications for Writers

Writer's Market, edited by Jane Koester and Paula Arnett Sandhage. The freelancer's bible, containing 4,095 listings covering 8,577 paying markets. You'll learn the name and address of the publication, the name of the editor, the kind of material he wants and how much he'll pay to get it. Extra: "How to Break In," a new section in which the editor gives you tips on how to sell to his publication. 936 pp. $13.50.

The Craft of Interviewing, by John Brady. Everything you always wanted to know about asking questions, but were afraid to ask — from an experienced interviewer and editor of *Writer's Digest*. The most comprehensive guide to interviewing on the market. 256 pp. $7.95.

The Mystery Writer's Handbook, edited by Lawrence Treat. A howtheydunit to the whodunit, newly written and revised by members of the Mystery Writers of America. The four elements essential to the classic mystery. How to make the reader turn the page. How to keep him guessing until the last page. A clear and comprehensive handbook that takes the mystery out of mystery writing. 256 pp. $8.95.

A Guide to Writing History, by Doris Ricker Marston. How to track down Big Foot, or your family Civil War letters, or your hometown's last century, for publication and profit. Where to find pictures and illustrations. How to prepare a manuscript for publication. A timely handbook for history buffs and writers. 258 pp. $8.50.

The Confession Writer's Handbook, by Florence K. Palmer. A stylish and informative guide to getting started and getting ahead in the confessions. Palmer, a veteran confessor, discusses the problems of confessions — and their solutions — as if she were sitting across the kitchen table from you. How to start a confession and carry it through. How to take an insignicant event and make it significant. 171 pp. $6.95.

A Complete Guide to Marketing Magazine Articles, by Duane Newcomb. "Anyone who can write a clear sentence can learn to write and sell articles on a consistent basis," says Newcomb (who has published well over 3,000 articles). Here's how. 248 pp. $6.95.

Writing Popular Fiction, by Dean R. Koontz. How to write mysteries, suspense thrillers, science fiction, Gothic romances, adult fantasy, Western and erotica. The difference between a Big Sexy Novel and a Rough Sexy Novel, and where the fortune is. Here's an inside guide to lively fiction, by a lively novelist. 232 pp. $7.95.

The Creative Writer, edited by Aron Mathieu. This book opens the door to the real world of publishing. Packed with inspiration, techniques, and ideas for writers. Plus inside tips from Maugham, Caldwell, Purdy and others. 416 pp. $6.95.

One Way to Write Your Novel, by Dick Perry. For Perry, a novel is 200 pages. Or, two pages a day for 100 days. Then he starts his next novel. And you can start — and finish — *your* novel, with the help of this step-by-step guide taking you from the blank sheet to the polished page. 138 pp. $6.95.

(Prices subject to change without notice.)
Writer's Digest, 9933 Alliance Road, Cincinnati, Ohio 45242